I0820554

THE ICONIC TROPICAL HOUSE

THE ICONIC TROPICAL HOUSE

PATRICK BINGHAM-HALL

With over 350 illustrations

CONTENTS

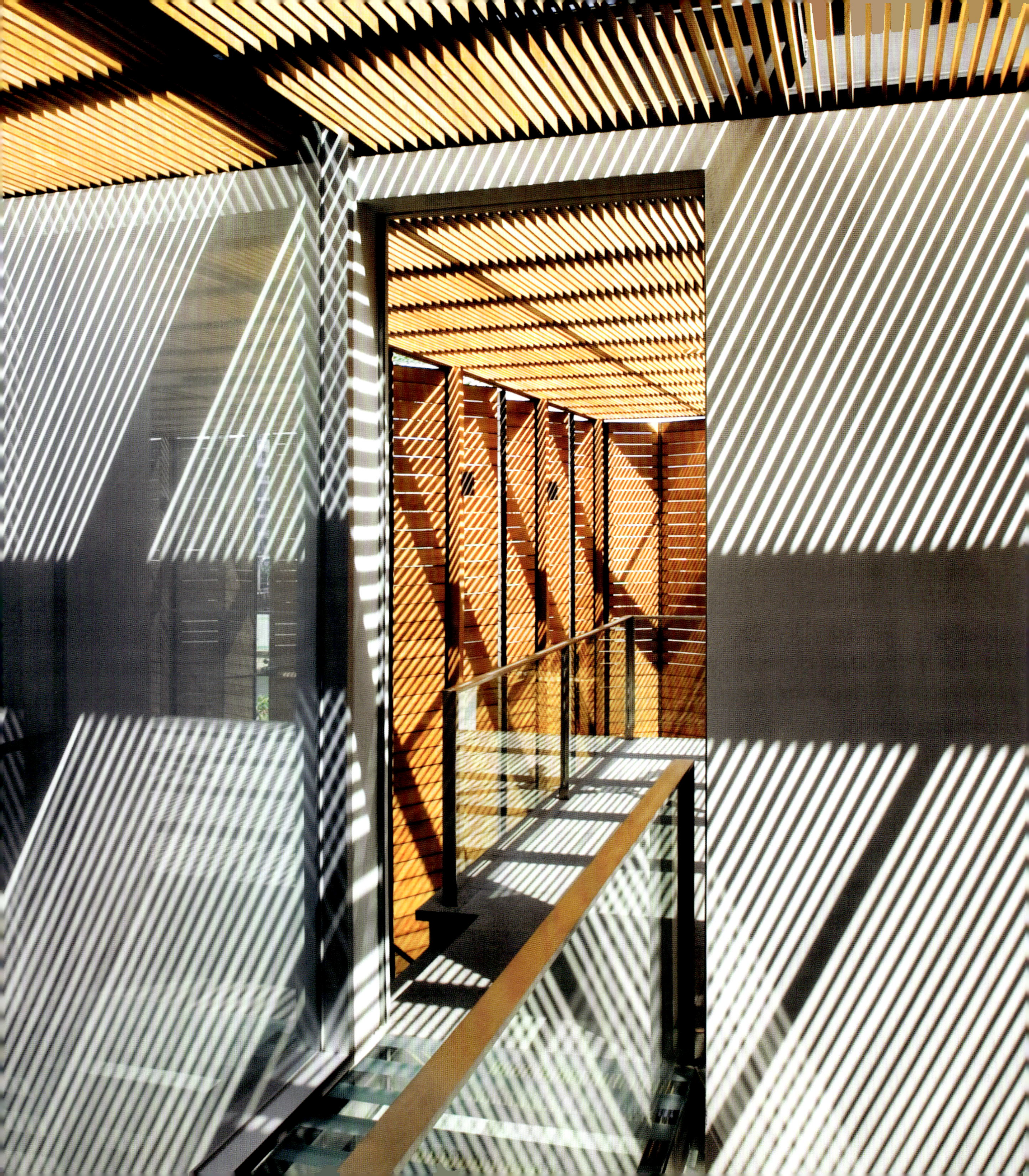

THERE'S NOTHING NEW UNDER THE SUN

The architecture shown in this book was designed and built over the last fifty years in a culturally diverse but climatically interconnected region: a tropical tapestry of monsoonal fecundity bookended by the parched fringes of India's northwest and the sunburnt aridity of the Australian outback. As acknowledged in the formal tomes, there has always been architecture here, but it has been that of the grand civilizations: the monuments of the Moghuls, the Khmer and the Majapahit, the stupas of Bagan, and the temples of Angkor and Borobudur. But what of the ephemeral and the vernacular? Those houses built from timber, bamboo, thatch, local stones and mud, those of a type that Bernard Rudofsky succinctly categorized as 'architecture without architects'.

Erected over millennia, across the fertile plains, and throughout the jungles and the islands, the vernacular methods of construction were characterized by what we might perceive as an exaggeration of proportion, but they were simply predicated upon practicality and efficiency in the face of stifling heat and torrential rain. The grandiose roofs and overhangs of the houses of the Minangkabau (in Sumatra) and the Toraja (in Sulawesi) have a graphically scaled extravagance of form, and they possess an 'expressionist' aesthetic, one that was primarily determined by necessity, by the imperative for optimal environmental performance. In the twenty-first century, it might be observed that in the name of ethical architectural practice, some things remain the same. In the tropics, there is nothing new under the sun.

The houses included in this book are located in India, Sri Lanka, Thailand, Malaysia, Vietnam, Singapore, Indonesia and (tropical) Australia. There has long been a degree of connectivity between the architectural histories of these nations, and despite the myriad inequities and the disparities, a geographically/climatically discrete process of cross-fertilization is ongoing: theoretical, practical and occasionally experimental.

In typological terms, the history of vernacular architecture in Southeast Asia has really been the story of the roof. As the anthropologist, Roxana Waterson, points out in her documentation of the Indonesian islands, 'One of the most striking features of architectural style in this part of the world is the enormous predominance of roof over wall. Whereas in the history of Western architecture, the wall is an essential element of built form, many of the buildings of Indonesian society have no walls at all, but consist entirely of roof, enclosing a pile-built platform.'[1] And, of course, this was not just an Indonesian thing. For millennia, the inhabitants of Southeast Asia had no concept of demographic delineation, never mind stylistic categorization: they were simply dealing with topographical and climatic exigencies with what they had at hand. All across tropical Asia, houses built from timber had that 'expressionist' quality – the gable roofs of Thailand, Malaysia and Sri Lanka, the spreading thatched roofs of the longhouses in Vietnam and the island of Borneo – that was quite wonderfully ephemeral. These structures were never built to last, the materials had a short shelf life and there was something personal: there was an existential intimacy you might say, with a dwelling that may not outlast you.

Across the sun-baked expanses of the Indian subcontinent and northern Australia, the notion of vernacular architecture was not quite so formalized. Rocks, sand and scrubby trees did not lend themselves to 'cost-effective' ornamental construction, and sites were generally very exposed. Indian houses were essentially 'lean-tos', built from timber, mud plaster, bamboo

OPPOSITE Ernesto Bedmar Architects, Cove Way House, Singapore, 2010.
ABOVE Minangkabau House, Sumatra, *c.* 1900–20.

and thatch (as many still are). The dwellings of Australia's indigenous precolonial inhabitants might also be described as lean-tos, built in the main from bark and tree trunks, and they were transitory, 'tents' if you like – temporary accommodation for nomadic people. The domestic architecture of India and Australia, as we now know it, was directed by British colonization – the rural homestead was more or less an antipodean bungalow – and a distinctive typology emerged, one that made the most of meagre resources and had a rudimentary dignity. Non-urban Australians built houses, sheds and public buildings from 'timber and tin', while Indians were more inclined to use bricks, tiles, mud and stone, and many of the most venerable recent houses in both countries can be recognized as direct descendants. In this book, one might point to Wall House by Anupama Kundoo (see p. 74), Nisarga by Wallmakers (see p. 228), Rozak House by Troppo (see p. 24) and Carpenter Hall House by Russell Hall (see p. 46).

However indubitably virtuous it might be to frame contemporary architecture in the context of vernacular histories, it must also be acknowledged that each nation referred to in this book was under the thumb of the Europeans for a considerable length of time. The colonial processes of adaptation, assimilation and regional iteration formed – enacted – the templates for town planning and residential construction.

Literally meaning 'of Bengal', the bungalow – a breezy and spacious single-storey dwelling for the expatriate officials of the East India Company – was first seen in the late-seventeenth century. The subsequent stylistic variations that spread across colonial settlements and plantations of southern Asia established an archetypal image of the languid tropical lifestyle: drowsing on the verandah beneath slowly twirling fans, somewhere out there in the steamy heat of the jungle. As to whether the bungalow should now be seen as a generically colonial or a specifically localized typology, the answer probably lies somewhere in-between. Which could also be said of the stylistic and structural twists and turns displayed by the teak houses of Thailand, the elevated Malay houses, the shophouses of the Straits Settlements and the, until recently ubiquitous, kampong houses.

Broadly speaking, the architecture of the colonial pre-modernist era was contextually appropriate, uniformly charming and occasionally beguiling. Somewhat inadvertently, and as dictated by non-architectural considerations, the post-colonial air-conditioned paths to modernity appeared to revoke the spirit of ingenuous construction and its quaintly endemic evocation of place. When the aesthetic limits of standardized modernism became increasingly apparent and the strictures became increasingly untenable, the intrinsic delights of living in a tropical house, which one might suggest are unsurpassed, were rediscovered. This book sets out to chart the courses that were taken by a wonderfully disparate range of architects.

THE BEATIFIC HOUSE

One of the largest houses featured in this book is, in effect, not much more than a great verandah. Perched above one of those gorgeous gorges that plunge through the rice fields of Bali, the Bond House (see p. 148) was not built as an imposition, but as part of a vista, or experience, that can only be described as sublime. The views, the landscape and the microclimate, are sensuous, exotic and beatific – they are too good to be true. And one is consummately immersed in the idyllic ambience; there is no 'architecture' to get in the way. Yet, almost imperceptibly, there is architecture, and therein

Anupama Kundoo Architects, Wall House, Auroville, India, 2000.

Wallmakers, Nisarga, Angamaly, India, 2023.

Troppo, Rozak House, Lake Bennett, Australia, 2000.

A colonial bungalow at Goodwood Hill, Singapore, 1910.

Alexis Dornier, Bond House, Bali, Indonesia, 2020.

C. Anjalendran, Malalasekera House, Colombo, Sri Lanka, 2011.

lies the essence of designing for paradise. Ingenuity or expression cannot be taken too far: the architecture should not constitute an intervention.

In the tropics, the fundamental motivation of the architect is to harness and calibrate the environmental determinants of the site, both the serendipitous pleasures and the inherent vicissitudes. On the one hand, the conditions for liveability – shade, shelter, ventilation – must be optimized, while on the other, a house needs to withstand the pouring rain, the rapid processes of weathering and the undesirable incursions from the natural world. That is the 'parti' of tropical architecture: revel in the idyll and repel the unwanted, not to mention the hazardous. Every house in this book can be 'read', can be understood, in this manner. In those parts of the world where the climate is more benign and accommodating, an architect can take liberties, but here in the tropics, a refusal to adhere to the prerequisites means that a house (and its residents) will not last very long.

The constraints of a site, particularly in built-up urban areas, form another set of determinants. As the Sri Lankan architect C. Anjalendran explains, 'Beneath the tropical sun, if the breadth of a house is more than 30 feet [9 metres], it will be too dark to live. You need to have courtyards to provide daylight and cross-ventilation.' Anjalendran studied under Geoffrey Bawa (see p. 84) and collaborated with him for many years, and if Bawa is to be venerated for one specific strategy out of all his accomplishments, it could well be his early career rejection of the then-prevalent bungalow type in the city of Colombo, replacing it with the courtyard house. Surrounded by verandahs and gardens, the solid-block plan of the bungalow took up a lot of space, which was becoming a rather precious commodity in the twentieth-century city. Quite simply, the insertion of an internal courtyard meant that the garden could be relocated within the house, thus obviating the need for an over-large site while providing a set of very sprightly living spaces. The idea was not exactly unprecedented, but the formal implementation of the courtyard house became an architectural standard across tropical Asia, to the point where, as a characteristic typology, it has now become almost invisible. Anjalendran himself has appropriated and manipulated that introspective spatial configuration to conjure up what might be termed as houses without architecture: 'I do not like decorative architecture. I expose the structure as far as possible, and I do not cheat. A house should display the lives of the occupants, not the architects.'

REVERSING THE CYCLE

The lands of southern Asia and northern Australia have been occupied for thousands of years without the destruction of natural ecosystems, the eradication of entire species of wildlife, or raising the levels of greenhouse gas emissions. In comparison with Western civilizations, the region was a latecomer to the anthropogenic era – industrialization and urban sprawl only really got underway in the mid- to late-twentieth century – but the processes of modernization have nonetheless repurposed the ecosystems swiftly and dramatically, while contributing ever-increasingly to the escalation of global warming. It is now estimated that approximately fifty percent of global greenhouse gas emissions are created by building construction and maintenance, and, given that much of tropical Asia is already suffering from deadly heatwaves and widespread flooding (the all-too-real consequences of climate change), the continuing cycle of build and build is fatefully veering toward disaster. Can the cycle be reversed? And if so, what role might architecture conceivably play? The answer to the latter question is 'quite a lot'. Governments, town planners and property developers have always looked to architects as the problem solvers; for better or worse, architects have always played a vanguard role.

In the tropics, the notion of 'reversing the cycle' is quite straightforward. It simply comprises a reversion to the basics, to the fundamentals of localized, context-specific, environmentally aware construction, which had been practised without aforethought before modernization and technological advance. Each of the houses shown in this book, even those that were 'pre-greenie, pre-environmentalist', have sustainability and passive design principles embedded in their intentions, as did the bungalows, the kampong houses and the Australian homesteads of a bygone age. Guz Wilkinson (see p. 164), who for thirty years has been designing homes in Singapore that are as notable for their gardens as for their architecture, states that 'It's so easy. It's so simple. You just need cross-ventilation, overhangs, plants and water bodies. You can attribute that to learning from the vernacular, but really... it's just common sense.'

For much of the twentieth century, landscape design was neglected, if not actively spurned, by the commandments of modernist architecture. In its greatly impassioned and high-minded beginnings, modernism had been in thrall to the machine, and by extension, to the vanquishing of the natural world. For several decades in tropical Asia, in a part of the world where nature grows more quickly and verdantly than any other, that modernist tenet held sway, but as the built environment and the qualities of existence have grown ever-more dour, landscape has been resurgent.

Ng Seksan, a landscape architect, engineer, property developer, architect/designer and regeneration specialist based in Kuala Lumpur, states unequivocally that, 'Softscape is all that matters in architecture these days, the forms and the beauty are in the trees and nature. The hardscape and the new buildings, they're not the architecture anymore.' Over a period of twenty years, he has built and/or assembled a series of houses or retreats, known as 'Sekepings' (see p. 266), which adopted a parti of 'reconfigure, renovate, recycle', wherein sustainability and environmental integration were fundamental, they were taken for granted. In spirit, his thoughts and outlook echo those of Laurie Baker (see p. 206), who confided in a 1986 interview that, 'I learn my architecture by watching what ordinary people do; in any case it's always the cheapest and the simplest.'[2] Back in the 1940s, Baker had been advised by none other than Mahatma Gandhi to only use materials that had been sourced within five miles of a building's location. Cheap and affordable, and sustainable.

THE ARCHITECTURE OF NOW

The architecture shown in this book, that of the tropical house in southern Asia and northern Australia, is only a recent phenomenon. The image of a tropical house has long been familiar to us, but it was something of a romantic notion: a fictional archetype and a colonial motif. To be sure, many fine houses were built between the late seventeenth and early twentieth centuries – from Bombay (now Mumbai) through to Penang and Surabaya, and down to Brisbane – and they were generally bungalows, elegantly and finely tuned with a neoclassical bent, as laid out in the imperial 'pattern books'. After the Second World War, something of an interregnum in regionally identifiable architecture was to follow (a circumstance that was a reflection of geopolitical

Guz Architects, Water Courtyard House, Singapore, 2022.

Seksan Design, Sekeping Jugra, Kuala Lumpur, Malaysia, 2016.

Laurie Baker, Isavasyam, Trivandrum, India, 1998.

Eaton & Bates, Cremorne, Brisbane, Australia, 1906.

imperatives in the post-colonial era), and there was little of enduring interest, apart from a series of public buildings – most notably in India – that took their cues from Le Corbusier and Oscar Niemeyer in particular.

An initial reinstatement of tropicality took place in northern Australia, where a group of Brisbane-based architects 'took to the bush' in the early 1970s. They embraced the environment rather than taming it, and they advocated a return to the expediency and affordability of the 'timber and tin' method of construction of nineteenth-century Queensland. Two of the architects, Russell Hall (see p. 46) and Rex Addison (see p. 50), worked in Papua New Guinea for several years and returned to Brisbane with the fundamentals for tropical design ingrained. As Addison recalls, 'The problems of working in PNG clarified a number of architectural issues for me. The vocabulary of the modern movement, distilled and pure, had little or no message in a country so far from the "Mediterranean cradle".'[3]

A simultaneous reawakening was taking place in Bali, where another pair of Australian architects – Peter Muller and Kerry Hill (see p. 108) – met up with Geoffrey Bawa in the early 1970s at Donald Friend's Batujimbar compound. Bawa had to all intents and purposes 'invented' tropical resort architecture several years previously with his Bentota Beach Hotel in Sri Lanka, and after his accumulated wisdom had been absorbed, the two Australians went on to design a series of resorts that established an enduring identity for tropical architecture in the region. Muller was fixated by an adherence to traditional architecture and craftsmanship, while Hill was more inclined to the 'Bawa-esque' fusion of tropicality with modernist form-making. That impetus and their degree of innovation had an abiding impact upon domestic architecture, while for the most part, resort design itself became formulaic and almost comically clichéd.

The no-nonsense attitude of the Brisbane architects spread northwest, to the maverick partnership of Troppo in Darwin, and then, perhaps most significantly (if not realized by the protagonists at the time), to Jimmy Lim (see p. 54) in Kuala Lumpur. Lim had studied in Sydney, and returned to Malaysia in the 1970s, intent upon rekindling the spirit and environmental performance of the kampong houses in which he had grown up in Penang. That he did, with a set of singular and intrinsically flamboyant timber houses that had nothing in common with the architectural trends of the 1970s and 1980s: 'I was way ahead of my time. It wasn't called sustainable back then, I was simply being efficient and frugal.... My architecture was expressive, but that was simply a manifestation of its functionality. And right from the start, I did not want to disturb the natural environment.'

The residents of tropical Asia were becoming increasingly affluent, and an emergent middle class could now consider commissioning dream homes. This was an incremental and ongoing process, beginning with Singapore in the 1980s, and, by and large, the architecture was not adventurous or noticeably tropical. But the seeds had been sown, and looking back now, it can be seen that the two strands – the expressiveness and structural honesty of the work that originated in Brisbane, and the Bawa-esque tropicality of the resort architecture – directly or indirectly inspired much that followed, culturally and philosophically, as much as architectonically.

In the 1990s, the domestic architecture of Singapore was widely publicized (a first for the region), and it was, to an extent, locally revered and highly influential. In terms of its performance and environmental intention, the architecture was rigorously and endemically tropical, but it did not look conspicuously tropical: there was a distinct demarcation between house and landscape, and some architects appeared to have a curious aversion to the use of eaves and the broad overhanging roof. The Asian iteration of 'tropical modernism' had been set in place by Bawa, who had trained at the Architectural Association in London during the 1950s, and it presented something of an aesthetic conundrum, one that lingers on in Singapore. However, the architectural program incorporated in the best work was a game-changer: the structure and the plans were clearly and graphically predicated upon sustainability and passive design.

Tropically expressive architecture was to flower across Southeast Asia, often unexpectedly as a series of 'one-offs', and the challenge was to avoid cliché and reiteration. It goes without saying that many fell into that trap, and an inherent dilemma was that of vernacular appropriation. It was pretty much impossible not to mimic the expression of the time-honoured forms of traditional climatically attuned architecture, so then, how to assert a contemporary expression? The 'iconic' houses have been the most tectonically interesting, those where the articulation of materials defined the work: the combinations of timber and stone; the weathering properties of off-form concrete; the patina of rusting metal; the striations of battened screens; the stark delineations of white-painted concrete; the crafted tactility of brickwork; and planting as façade components.

Design Unit, Bamboo House, Kuala Lumpur, Malaysia, 2009.

ARCHITECTURE AND THE CITY

The tropical house is, however, not solely defined by the creation of the beautiful and the idyllic. Southern Asia can only be called paradise by a lucky few. Nearly three billion people live here, and nearly half live in extremely hot, overcrowded, malfunctioning cities. Architectural reactions to those conditions have been fermenting since the late 1990s, when the size, significance and wealth of the middle class had reached a critical mass. The evolution of tropical house design has been accompanied by an *urban* architecture, wherein the realities of megacity life are not to be blithely ignored, not to be left behind at the gates of the estate or on the freeway out of town. Perhaps the most potent, and occasionally confronting, architecture to have emerged in equatorial Asia is to be found deep within the living bodies of the cities, in the landscapes where culture and civilization rise and fall.

A wide range of architects have enacted a policy of adapt and re-use, or they set about designing houses that have an umbilical attachment to their place in the city, and by extension, to their microclimate and environment. Aside from the virtuousness of the architectural programs and their environmental performance, the immersion within and the embrace of local context provided a visual and cultural identity for neighbourhoods, and even for the city itself. One is almost required to visualize Jakarta as the background and source in order to understand Andra Matin's architecture (see p. 256), as with Kuala Lumpur for Kevin Low (see p. 278) and Ng Seksan, Bangkok for Boonserm Premthada (see p. 272) and Boonlert Hemvijitraphran (see p. 234), and Hanoi and Ho Chi Minh City for Đoàn Thanh Hà (see p. 262) and Vo Trong Nghia (see p. 222). The site-specific works of those architects would look out of place in any other urban environment, and with their understanding of and devotion to the local, they have reinterpreted and redefined the image of their host cities.

Gfab Architects, Samujana, Koh Samui, Thailand, 2014.

H&P Architects, Brick Cave, Hanoi, Vietnam, 2017.

studioMilou, Nassim House, Singapore, 2020.

THINGS ARE NOT WHAT THEY WERE

As with the waterways that meander across the deltas of Asia's great rivers, the courses of tropical architecture that were set in motion some fifty or so years ago are braided, forever intertwining. Within such a short time span, the paradigm shifts of culture and context across the region have been rapid, and occasionally uncontrollable. Tropical architecture's brief period of emergence and evolution has embodied several contradictions – environmental, social and stylistic – which have been continually redirected by geopolitical transformations, not to mention the tangible impacts of climate change. The projects featured in this book should, above all, be viewed as a reflection of those processes. Things are most definitely not what they were in tropical Asia.

BRISBANE, DARWIN AND JIMMY LIM

'The one certain thing about going north in Australia is that the further north you go, the further north you want to go.'

CHARMIAN CLIFT[1]

The climate classification analysts might insist otherwise but, as anyone who has spent quality time in its hilly environs and on its sleepy riverfront will attest, Brisbane is a tropical city in all but name. The summers are hot and humid, and they seem to last for at least half the year, the winters are balmy and benign, the vegetation is bountiful and fecund, the early housing stock was built sparingly from timber and perched on stilts, the residents are noticeably unhurried and the lifestyle, you might say, tends toward the laidback. Yet for most of the twentieth century, the local arbiters of taste and governance looked toward the temperate south rather than the tropical north, and the city's architecture comprised stolid reiterations of that found in Sydney and Melbourne, whose buildings were hand-me-downs from overseas in the first place – Brisbane was thus two rungs down the ladder from London and Los Angeles. That rigid adherence to the doctrines of modernism looked totally out of place, both in the streets of the business district and out in the leafy expanses of the suburbs, but the post-war years were those of the cultural cringe – the belief that anything in Australia could only be judged by standards set elsewhere – and Brisbane could not admit to its individuality, never mind its tropicality. And to make things worse, Robin Boyd, a Melburnian advocate for imported modernism who held great sway in the 1950s, made this pronouncement: 'The north Australian traditional vernacular, disparaged today by scientist and stylist alike, is living numbered days in Brisbane.'[2] He was effectively de-romanticizing the virtues of a localized architecture and blithely ignoring the benefits of what we now refer to as sustainable construction. This provincial outlook was sadly indicative of an environmental and aesthetic naïvete that trundles on in Australia to this day.

Freed by the counterculture ethos of the late 1960s from the strictures of such imported conventions, an assortment of Brisbane-educated architects ventured into the bushland of the city's surrounds in the early 1970s with a strategy of environmental assimilation rather than confrontation. And, apart from anything else, that moment of (re)awakening constituted a tangible reversion to 'north Australia traditional vernacular'. It was a seminal moment, not so much for Brisbane itself, or indeed for the rest of Australia, but in the long run for the advancement of tropical architecture itself.

Two of the young architects, Russell Hall (see p. 46) and Rex Addison (see p. 50), headed (independently) to Papua New Guinea (PNG) to set up practice, and the buildings they produced there were indeed pioneering, even though they went more or less unnoticed by the architectural establishment. The lessons they learnt were brought back to Brisbane a few years later, when they both designed houses that were noticeably tropicalized. As Addison recalls: 'The problems of working in PNG clarified a number of architectural issues for me. The vocabulary of the modern movement, distilled and pure, had little or no message in a country so far from the "Mediterranean cradle". Functionally and semantically, a local building language had to be evolved. These preoccupations continued when I returned to Australia.'[3]

In 1975, Addison built a charmingly reticent house for his young family on a thickly vegetated sloping site in the suburb of Taringa, and he engaged in an almost laconic relationship with the natural realities of its context. 'The use of timber was sensible: it was an abundant material with a low thermal mass. Coping with a subtropical climate (mild, pleasant winter and a long hot summer) was made easier by adopting this light framing technique. I wanted to use these building forms and extend their meaning to produce another "generation" of house types.'[4] Hall designed a collection of really quite radical buildings in Papua New Guinea, and they were followed by a series of equally arresting houses on the coast north of Brisbane and its hinterland. Boroko Office and Shops (1978, Port Moresby) was a remarkable soaring edifice, sheathed in corrugated iron with curling leaf-like awnings, and it formed a consummate exercise in passive climatic performance – shade, ventilation, shelter and no air-conditioning. His own house on a bushland site near Buderim (1982), north of Brisbane, was a progenitor for an ongoing breed of ostensibly informal shacks shaped by the hands of others (trained and semi-trained), and Hall was proud to publicize that the house was never finished, which did not appear to matter to him. The three living spaces fan out to the views as facetted semicircles, and the columns are

ABOVE Rex Addison, Addison House 1, Brisbane, Australia, 1975.

ABOVE Russell Hall Architects, Boroko Office and Shops, Port Moresby, Papua New Guinea, 1978.

formed from upturned tree trunks, with the root formations serving as the crowning capitals – Hall refers to this 'classical' arrangement as 'a new Australian order'.

Along with Hall and Addison, several other architects in the Brisbane region – notably Gabriel Poole, John Mainwaring and Lindsay and Kerry Clare – would soon rise to prominence and acclaim, but within Australia, their buildings were seen as 'lightweight structures' rather than tropical designs, and the catchphrase of 'touching the ground lightly' neatly encapsulated the common essence of a nationwide genre. Beyond the self-referential confines of the Australian architecture pool, the direct and immediate influence of the 'Brisbane School' in particular was profound, if curiously unheralded, and a north-bound process of tropical cross-fertilization took shape in the 1980s. In Darwin, way up in that sparsely settled, very hot and humid and/or arid part of Australia known as the Top End, a couple of young Adelaide-trained architects – Phil Harris and Adrian Welke – set up shop in 1980. Not wishing to mislead the marketplace, they named their practice Troppo, and subsequent to their studies of housing types in the region, they self-published a minor classic, a small book packed with cartoonlike sketches, which was entitled *Punkahs and Pith Helmets: Good Principles of Tropical House Design* (1982).

Troppo had four fundamental principles: the promotion of cooling breezes; ventilation by convection; reducing radiation of heat; and the sheltering of walls and openings. As Philip Goad was to point out many years later, 'With these principles, Troppo in effect laid down ground rules for the development of regionally and climatically responsible architecture.'[5] One of Troppo's most pragmatic and most influential prototypes was erected in 1982 – it was named the 'Green Can' in honour of the Victoria Bitter beer can, and comprised two living zones set apart by a breezeway and sheltered by skillion roofs that sloped steeply away from each other. From the outset, Troppo proclaimed its admiration for the work of Glenn Murcutt, and somewhat slyly introduced his detailing and finesse to its outwardly rough-and-ready houses, but it was with Russell Hall and his 'when in doubt, just do it' attitude that the practice had most in common, and it was proud to acknowledge his influence. Over the next two decades, Troppo's architectural output in the Northern

ABOVE Troppo, Lawler House (under construction), Darwin, Australia, 1984.

Territory was prolific, and the practice eventually became an Australia-wide operation.

By virtue of its geographic location (it is rumoured that on a very clear day, you can just about glimpse Indonesia from Darwin), Troppo was ineluctably drawn into a regional web of occasional architectural discourse and a concomitant exchange of ideas. One of its earliest acquaintances was Jimmy Lim, a Malaysian architect who had gone to high school and university in Sydney, before setting up practice in Kuala Lumpur (see p. 54). As to whether his university education had any formal bearing upon his work, Lim remains unconvinced, but he returned to Malaysia with open eyes and a very clear idea of what he wanted to do and what his country's architectural expression might consist of. Lim spent his childhood in a kampong house in Penang – raised above the ground with an unobstructive well-ventilated internal layout that embraced the tropical climate – and he wished to revert to those principles and their attendant pleasures. Lim's predilection may now appear to be unremarkable, but it was almost revolutionary forty years ago. In the 1980s and 1990s, he designed a collection of houses that emphatically reinstated the fundamental principles and techniques for regionally (and culturally) appropriate construction, along with a vivacious and all-pervasive delight in craft and ornamentation, and the use of timber in particular. Lim's enthusiastic renewal of the pleasures of tropical lifestyle as a hedonistic experience had an impact comparable to that of Peter Muller's design for the Oberoi Hotel in Bali a decade earlier, and not coincidentally, he repeatedly declared that all he wanted to do was build houses that were private resorts.

Jimmy Lim's houses were game-changers. Apart from anything else, his highly expressive reassertion of vernacular form was appropriated by others, and duly filtered, to provide Southeast Asia with a fresh identity in its public architecture – one that was no longer a regionally inflected pastiche of Oscar Niemeyer and Edward Durell Stone. In regard to domestic architecture, his direct influence was not so conspicuous. The trouble with doing what he did was that once he had done it, there were not many other ways to do it – a Jimmy Lim-type house will always look like a Jimmy Lim house. His indirect influence, however, was considerable, as he had squarely placed tropicality back on the table, and with that came an assortment of social, cultural and environmental considerations (dilemmas) that had remained dormant during Southeast Asia's 'march to modernity' period. The next generation of Malaysian architects – spearheaded by Kevin Low and Ng Seksan – had a markedly different approach to the use of materials, the tectonics of design and to stylistic appropriation, but they were essentially taking the next step forward from the work of Lim.

Meanwhile, back in Brisbane, the evolution of tropical (or subtropical) architecture continued to flourish until the early twenty-first century, when curiously and unaccountably, the whole thing pretty much evaporated. Russell Hall designed Carpenter Hall House in 1985 (see p. 46), which still stands resplendent as one of the great landmarks to expressive tropicality, and followed that with the wonderfully resolved Judge House (1987) on an island off the north Queensland coast – 'We could not further weaken the established environment...the house should be an accepted immigrant, not an imposed alien'.[6] Addison had a 'second wind' in the mid-1990s, with a sequence of projects – including his own house and studio (see p. 50) – that displayed a mastery of how to visualize section and plan as a holistic entity, as a 'machine for breathing', so to speak.

Gabriel Poole had devoted his practice to the production of housing prototypes that could be quickly assembled on the site of your choosing, but in a nation fixated above all else with the enduring commercial value of property, his vision was ultimately too unrealistic, too quixotic to succeed as a business venture. Poole's process, however, did produce some conspicuously innovative pieces of 'lightweight' tropical architecture built from steel, as

ABOVE Jimmy Lim, House (and Research Centre) at Taman Seputeh, Kuala Lumpur, Malaysia, 1978 onward.

seen in the elemental and extremely elegant delineations of the Gloster House (1984) and his own house at Lake Weyba (1996). With the Rosebery House (1997) and the Mooloomba House (1998; see p. 36), the partnership of Brit Andresen and Peter O'Gorman composed two eloquent 'essays' on the delights and virtues of the exposed timber frame, which were highly acclaimed and widely publicized, and did much to foster the image of a city blessed with a seductively tropical demeanour. Finally, to round off Brisbane's period of pre-eminence with a lingering legacy, the mercurial practice of Donovan Hill produced a collection of houses and public buildings at the turn of the century that, even at the smallest scale, utilized a monumentality of mass and void as a way to respond to the climate and context (see p. 42). In doing so, they markedly diverged from the organically attuned and innately deferential approach of their predecessors.

ABOVE Gabriel Poole, Lake Weyba House, Weyba Downs, Australia, 1996.

TOP Andresen O'Gorman, Rosebery House, Brisbane, Australia, 1997.
ABOVE Donovan Hill, C House, Brisbane, Australia, 1998.

ROZAK HOUSE

2000
LAKE BENNETT, AUSTRALIA
TROPPO

'The "travellers camp" introduces the idea of a minimalist architecture in achieving a culturally distinct environmental fit, a level of comfort and a phenomenological position in the cultural landscape; the idea of an architecture without buildings,' explains Paul Memmott, continuing, 'From this there follows a definition of architecture which is more appropriate for the cultural circumstances of many aboriginal people – environment contexts.'[1]

In 1980, Phil Harris and Adrian Welke, two young architects who had recently graduated from the University of Adelaide, set up practice in Darwin, the frontier town at Australia's northernmost edge. The Top End, as it is known, is a place where the weather is occasionally very wild and the climate is either wet or dry or both, and it is always hot. Far removed from any kind of mainstream and unfettered by the mores of establishment, Harris and Welke applied themselves diligently and inventively to the implementation of environmentally appropriate architecture in the region. As an immediate indication of just how cheerfully and unpretentiously they set about their work (and their lives), they named their practice Troppo, and although it took an inordinate amount of time for the news to filter through, they eventually established a maverick presence in an Australian architectural scene that was then absorbed by postmodern deconstructivist theorizing. (Once Troppo took to the stage at a seminar in Sydney wearing broad-brimmed hats with corks attached, and cracking open cans of beer mid-recital.) They were, however, very serious and perceptive practitioners and communicators, and they helped to change the course of tropical architecture well beyond the Top End of Australia.

Troppo effectively set out the fundamental principles for tropical design and construction – they self-published books that detailed those principles, and they built and built, to the point where visitors to Darwin could take the Troppo tour. In essence, their architecture marked a return to the elevated lightweight houses of the Top End that, prior to the arrival of Cyclone Tracy in 1974, had formed the most efficient and comfortable way to live in the tropics. After the cyclone had blown most of those houses away, town planners and local builders understandably opted to stay close to the ground. To once again go lightweight, to build elevated houses that would catch all the breezes, Troppo went heavyweight, using rigid, robust and cyclone-proof steel frames.

LEFT View from the southern hillside, showing the three lightweight pavilions linked on a 'propeller' plan.

ABOVE View from the north. The pavilions are separated by an entry platform with a lookout tower.

In the late 1990s, Mike Rozak, an American computer programmer made the radical choice to abandon the suburbs of Seattle and relocate, all alone, to what might be described as the middle of nowhere, or in local parlance, the back of beyond. As a computer whizz-kid he could conduct his business most efficiently from wherever he liked, and he purchased 18 hectares (45 acres) of arid and scrubby land some 80 kilometres (50 miles) south of Darwin. As he explained, 'There's a lot of space out here. You don't feel crowded in.' On the edge of a rocky south-facing ridge that gazes out over a hot, hazy and pretty much untouched landscape, Troppo designed and quickly fabricated a house that stands as an archetype: a symbolic representation of an enduring Australian myth, that of the rugged, stoic settlers and their primitive structures, both equipped to withstand the extremities and privations of the outback.

From the winding track that leads up the hilltop, the house is first glimpsed as a skeletal blackened frame that blends into, if not mimics, the twisted and sparsely leaved trunks of the trees on the slope. It has an aerodynamic profile, likened by Rozak to an eagle about to take flight, and in purely structural terms, it looks like nothing so much as one of those old biplanes

ABOVE View from the east. The elevated pavilions soar above the rocky terrain of Australia's Top End.

ABOVE The entry platform is shielded by sheets of translucent polycarbonate.

parked on the tarmac, a boxy assemblage angled skyward. Three pavilions are linked on a plan that resembles a ceiling fan, and in order to stimulate as much airflow as possible through high vents and the gaps between the floorboards, the two bedroom wings have warped roofs while the living/dining pavilion is surmounted by a skillion (a roof with a single, sloping plane that runs from one side of a building to the other) that rears up to embrace the view. The house thus appears as a compound, or camp, tented by a canopy of corrugated Zincalume steel and translucent polycarbonate. Many of the walls are transparent, evanescent and unglazed – they are fly-screens, that is all – while the remainder, those in the private and service areas, are of perforated Zincalume, clad internally with plywood.

It might be tempting to regard the house as something of a folly, built for a man who was literally 'going troppo', but that was not the case. The place, the environment, the elemental lifestyle suited Mike Rozak, and he lived there with the equanimity he had anticipated, and had indeed sought, until his death in 2013. Insofar as a white man and white architects can go in reaching an understanding of a land that had existed in equilibrium for so long without their presence, it might be said quietly that this project covered quite some distance. It was a 'travellers camp', it did not significantly disturb its site, it can be folded up and moved on, and, in an anthropological sense, it does accord quite agreeably with Paul Memmott's notion of an architecture without buildings.

ABOVE The interior living spaces comprise a set of cross-ventilated verandahs with a panoramic view framed only by fly-screens.

ABOVE As with all Troppo's architecture in the Top End, the house is elevated well above the ground and built from cyclone-proof steel frames.

WOOI RESIDENCE

2003
SHAH ALAM, MALAYSIA
WOOI ARCHITECT

The early years of the twenty-first century saw the flowering of a well-considered Malaysian architecture, one where a reverence for local craftsmanship and form-making was newly defined by an architectonic discipline that steered well clear of mimicry and mawkishness. It was a contemporary vernacular, if you like, wherein the architecture was resolutely of its place yet underpinned by and imbued with an undeniably sophisticated (and worldly) intellectual rigour. Lok Kuang Wooi's design for his own house and studio was a remarkably inventive, not to say flamboyant, representation of this synthesis, and it was informed by his upbringing in rural Malaysia, his formal training in Australia and his subsequent tenure with Jimmy Lim – a seminal figure in the late-twentieth-century renaissance of tropical architecture. Lim's houses had most delightfully reasserted the joys of tropical expression and craftsmanship, but, and this is no criticism, he had not sought to integrate contemporary forms and details. Lim was not inclined to encourage modernity to interfere with his prelapsarian idyll.

Wooi cites the influence of Bruce Rickard and Richard Leplastrier, who had both taught him at university in Sydney, and it might be observed that his house – and indeed all his architecture – was directed by a confluence of Lim's tropicalized theatricality with the measured appreciation for materiality espoused by those two architects. Rickard and Leplastrier were members of the Sydney School, a loose grouping of architects that designed bushland houses notable for their raw and warm brickwork, and – especially in Leplastrier's case – the virtues of exposed timberwork. The architects of the Sydney School were unabashed devotees of Frank Lloyd Wright (and, at first hand, the houses of Walter Burley Griffin), and it is not difficult to discern that lineage in the spatial planning and organic configurations of the Wooi Residence.

Located on a sloping site in the southwest of Kuala Lumpur's metropolitan sprawl, the Wooi Residence is most emphatically anti-suburban despite the constrictions of its rectangular plot. The architecture is self-referential, taking the notion of a traditional tropical Malaysia as its context, and screening out suburban propinquity by means of slatted timber and copious

OPPOSITE The structure is a synthesis of traditional Malaysian form and a more contemporary organic architecture. **ABOVE** The timber ceiling of the master bedroom fans out as a leaf-like structure.

stands of bamboo. Sheltered beneath a soaring fan-shaped roof, which rises dramatically over the southern gardens, the three levels of the house have an open-ended flow, specifically calibrated to engender continuous cross-ventilation – horizontal, diagonal and vertical. That sense of movement, of kinetic circulation, is manifest in the spatial planning, whereby rooms, corridors and stairs are dancing to the same tune without discordance or hesitation and, by extension, so are the materials and the exposure to daylight. The mid-level family areas are connected to the bedrooms above and the studio below by stairwells in an alcove, which was formed by load-bearing columns and walls surfaced with fair-faced bricks. All the rooms look into or over the southern gardens, which splay out from a grand 'tiang seri' (or central post) that supports the wooden roof trusses. The vertiginous views of the house from the gardens reveal a curiously fortified aspect to the architecture, whereby the curving panoramic sweep of windows and screens is enclosed by what appears to be a set of brick turrets and battlements. Wooi's flair for such allusive referencing and asymmetrical composition is continued through the interior spaces, exemplified by the leaf-like structure of the timber ceilings and the syncopated rhythms of the walls and window frames.

Both internally and externally, a palette of brick and timber is all-pervasive, and the aesthetic is that of a stripped-back quasi-industrial rendition of the Sydney School and, ipso facto, of Frank Lloyd Wright. And oddly enough, this is where the contemporary vernacular becomes apparent, where an identifiably Malaysian spirit has stamped itself on the architecture. The materials are assembled and integrated in a manner that is raw, knowingly raw, which in itself forms an acknowledgment of the pointlessness of over-finessing in a tropical environment. And that, it might be contended, was a deliberated expression of a Malaysian aesthetic. Wooi's architecture, and that of several peers,[1] evinced a fresh invigorated pride in the oft-rambunctious local – both cultural and aesthetic – and that was a serendipitous moment, one to be cherished, and one that has already acquired a substantial legacy.

RIGHT Protected by a fan-shaped roof, the house rises dramatically over the southern gardens. Wooi used a 'tiang seri' central pole to support the roof.

OPPOSITE AND ABOVE Both internally and externally, a palette of brick and timber is all-pervasive. All three levels have an open-ended flow.

MOOLOOMBA HOUSE

1998
NORTH STRADBROKE ISLAND, AUSTRALIA
ANDRESEN O'GORMAN

In retrospect, it is interesting to note the degree to which the architecture of Brit Andresen and Peter O'Gorman was venerated for the seriousness of its intent, having an intellectual and tectonic program that was perhaps somewhat unlikely in the patently laissez-faire cultural context of Brisbane. It must be said, however, that both architects were very much part of a generational milieu whose dryly localized laconicism cloaked a rigorous and pedantic approach to an appropriate form of subtropical construction. The likes of Gabriel Poole, Lindsay and Kerry Clare, Rex Addison and Russell Hall were dogmatic, to the point of zealotry, in their research into and advocacy for the fundamentals of sustainable architecture and its expression. But the husband-and-wife partnership of Andresen and O'Gorman went even further. The couple were also full-time architectural academics and each of their completed projects was considered in pedagogical terms, as objects for research, hypothesis and

OPPOSITE AND ABOVE The ship-like proportions of the house thrust out from a narrow and densely treed site.

critical evaluation, and the concomitant publicity – which was quite extensive – was very much couched in those terms. All of which has possibly obscured an appreciation of their houses as imaginatively conceived and beautifully constructed pieces of tropical architecture.

Mooloomba House was built as their own getaway from Brisbane, on North Stradbroke Island, reached by a forty-minute ferry trip. Rather surprisingly, given its quite striking ambience of spaciousness and complexity, the house occupies a small site that is hemmed in by typically unpretentious holiday-house neighbours. The stately demeanour of the diminutive structure resulted from a very deliberate strategy of deceptive scaling, which was explained by the architects as 'deferring to the existing landscape, alluding to a mythical landscape, and creating a constructed landscape to intensify the place of the house in its wider setting. The evocation of a mythic landscape recalls elements of a child's tree house and the bower in Milton's *Paradise Lost*.'[1]

With negligible demarcation between indoor and outdoor spaces, this is a compound rather than a house, and the built forms quite simply merge with those of the gnarled and unruly banksias that splay upward from the sandy soils. The built forms are, however, far from unruly – they were meticulously composed and scrupulously assembled, according to Andresen O'Gorman's intention to 'explore the expressive capacity of hardwood in terms of its material properties, geometry and metaphor'.[2] This was realized by building frames that would 'counteract hardwood's excessive lateral movement by vertically laminating thin members of opposing grain. The frame components must fit together harmonically, as a skeletal structure, to make a whole.'[3] Throughout the two levels of the pavilions, an orchestrated sequence of black-stained battens, beams, columns and trusses forms a rhythmic ensemble occasionally relieved by 'naturally blonde' cypress poles and slats.

The influence, the legacy, of Andresen O'Gorman has in terms of built work, been less substantial than might have been anticipated. The practice's work has been accorded due import in architectural histories, but tangible typological reapplications have been thin on the ground. That could be explained by the intensity of their approach, and indeed their rhetoric. Perhaps they were a hard act to follow. And it must be said that Mooloomba House is probably a little too theoretical and domestically impractical – the circulation spaces are very narrow, and the upkeep would presumably become rather tiresome. However, a sister project, the Rosebery House at Highgate Hill, close to the centre of Brisbane, was built at the same time and

OPPOSITE The central dining room is distinguished by the structural and aesthetic arrangements of timber elements.

in the same architectural language, and it has since served well as a family home, with the stairways and corridors notably accommodating.

Perhaps the real conundrum results from the essential tropicality of Andresen O'Gorman's architecture, and this also applies to the practice's local peer group of the time. Architects could build like this in Brisbane, they could get away with skeletal structure and inside/outside spaces, but any further south – where most Australian architects work – that expression is simply not feasible. Most unfortunately, the nature of recent intellectual discourse and an inclination toward cultural homogenization have engendered an inverse trend, whereby the architecture of Sydney and Melbourne – cities with a temperate climate – now appears to set the tone for most construction elsewhere. And, as a corollary, it must also be observed that the work of Andresen O'Gorman, among others, has never really been portrayed internationally as tropical architecture (which it is), but as Australian – whatever that might mean in a land of such environmental and climatic extremes.

OPPOSITE AND ABOVE Andresen O'Gorman's intention was to 'explore the expressive capacities of hardwood in terms of its material properties, geometry and metaphor'.

D HOUSE

2001
BRISBANE, AUSTRALIA
DONOVAN HILL

As its star shone so brightly in the Australian architecture firmament at the close of the twentieth century, the Brisbane-based partnership of Brian Donovan and Timothy Hill seemed too good to be true, as indeed it was. Founded in 1992, the studio produced a slew of buildings at various scales that evinced both a singular aesthetic expression and an acute awareness of the idiosyncrasies of their subtropical settings, before merging with another practice in 2012. Donovan Hill's position in the context of a local and regional architecture was anomalous and, in a posthumous sense, rather intriguing. For most of the year, Brisbane is to all intents and purposes a tropical city, and from the early 1970s until the late 1990s, a collection of architects[1] working in the region established a type of architecture that revisited the traditions and environmental suitability of Queensland lightweight structures, those built from 'timber and tin'. That architecture was to become influential well beyond the confines of Southeast Queensland, spreading across Southeast Asia, but Donovan Hill was, as Philip Goad wrote at the time, 'the exception rather than the rule.... From the outset, the buildings had unusual aspirations; monumentality (mass) matched with "the makings of miniatures" through exquisite detail fragments (lightness); and the consistent investigation of a new spatial type for the climate – the ventilating and open-air "significant room" or space.'[2] Most curiously, however, Donovan Hill also marked a tangible termination to the processes of innovation and expression in Australian tropical architecture – they were not just the exception, they were the last hurrah.

Although diminutive, D House was possibly the most influential of all Donovan Hill's completed projects, and one of the explanations for this lies in their own assessment of its function and program: 'It may be used as a family house, but equally it may accommodate non-family residents, or someone working from home, or it could be an office or studio, or a shop, or a café.'[3] In other words, located in the inner-city suburb of New Farm, it felt like quite a 'public' house, and it could be viewed pretty much as a prototype for an adaptable all-purpose urban structure. Indeed, it quickly became apparent that nearly every chichi redevelopment in a rapidly gentrifying Brisbane would need to have a tribute to D House as a café or marketplace or boutique providore. The other reason for its popularity and usefulness was that, sited in the backyard of a house whose block of land had just been subdivided, it

OPPOSITE AND ABOVE The house has a narrow setback from the street. A long slot window with a sliding screen enables community engagement.

ABOVE AND OPPOSITE The architecture of the large inside/outside space alternates between timber and masonry, and between robust and ethereal.

had been (relatively) cheap to build – its architectonic elegance belied its constructional simplicity.

Lying low on its small rectangular block, the house is set back on its frontage by a heaped garden bed and a narrow pathway, and its stuccoed façade has a lengthy slot window through which the occupants can engage directly with life on the street. The window can be closed off by a sliding timber screen, and now that the trees have grown up, the immediate connection has been diffused but, at the time, it did look like a shop counter or servery; hence the café reference. The architects describe the main volume of the house as 'a continuous inside/outside space' – or as Goad would have it, 'the open-air significant room' – and the interior is both intricately detailed and artlessly articulated. The street-facing wall is thick, to protect from the western sun, and the fittings and the textures alternate between timber and masonry, and between robust and ethereal. Small openings are carved out of all the walls and the roof to stimulate air movement and illuminate the interior with flickering patches of sunshine that dance across the whitewashed surfaces.

Donovan Hill's architecture was very clever, in a formal sense and in terms of its planning and passive-energy strategies, but it was also very worldly and knowledgeable. The list of iconic references to be found in the practice's work is quite exhaustive – Wright, Scarpa, Aalto and so on – and due deference is also paid to an earlier generation of local architects who were inclined to a Mediterranean use of mass and masonry – John Dalton, James Birrell and Robin Gibson, among others. Donovan Hill synthesized those various influences to formulate and inspire an especially distinctive architecture that was both capricious and highly serviceable, and very much of its location: of a benign, laidback and discernibly tropicalized Brisbane.

CARPENTER HALL HOUSE

1985
BRISBANE, AUSTRALIA
RUSSELL HALL ARCHITECTS

For those wishing to categorize and evaluate the course of architecture over the last fifty years or so, especially as it pertains to the tropics, and to Australia and Southeast Asia in particular, the oeuvre of Russell Hall is of critical import. His name does not crop up very often in recent readings of architecture in the region – Hall paid scant attention to the fashions and theories emanating from Sydney and Melbourne, and that lack of interest was reciprocated – and many of his seminal works were built in Papua New Guinea, where they did not last very long in their intended condition.

Yet in purely pragmatic terms, his influence has been far-reaching. It was he who quite matter-of-factly demonstrated that the construction method that had sustained white settlers in the very hot parts of Australia could be tweaked, if not finessed, to serve as reputable, serviceable architecture. That form of construction was referred to as 'timber and tin', and while it was not exactly the traditional vernacular of northern Australia (that honour is reserved for the timber and bark of the original inhabitants), it was for a long time the only affordable way to build with readily available materials. The point here is that much of Australia's subsequent lack of architectural identity stems from an apparently immutable unwillingness to continue in that spirit of making something lyrical out of the local, the unadorned and the cost-effective. Modern Australian architects have, generally, preferred to apply a veneer of Euro-stylization – focusing on the finishes, not the form. Russell Hall blithely ignored that incongruity and the progeniture of his archetypes can now be seen all over the region, if not at the architectural award ceremonies.

As Hall recounts in regard to Carpenter Hall House, one of his most iconic structures: 'The idea of a small tower was canvassed with the client. She admitted to a "Rapunzel Complex". For those not familiar with the work of Freud, this is not a desire to grow long hair, but an inbuilt craving to live in a tower.' Hall's formidable and dare-we-say whimsical client happened to be his sister, Jennifer, and after gaining her approval to build the tower-house, he goes on to explain his preferred design and construction process: 'A myopic, cycloptic Quantity Surveying method was adopted. This seldom-used method is based on the philosophy, "Let's just start, somehow we'll make it".'[1]

The overriding geometry of the five-storey tower, both in plan and structure, was dodecagonal – that is to say that all the permutations were taken from the possibilities provided by a twelve-sided polygon. As Hall notes,

OPPOSITE AND ABOVE The five-storey timber-framed tower is enclosed by an exoskeleton of V-shaped sunshades-as-gutters.

twelve has a 'useful divisibility, inherent in the imperial system of measure but not found in the metric'.[2] Each of the floor plans was derived from a variation on that dodecagonal measure, as was the ascending array of gang-nailed timber frames, all subdivided to form a resolute system of modular bracing. The mighty timber-framed structure was then enclosed by an exoskeleton of V-shaped sunshades-as-gutters made from galvanized steel, and when the rain becomes a downpour, as it often does up here, the torrents cascading from those eaves provide quite an audiovisual spectacle. The house is perched on a small south-facing hillside in Wilston, 5 kilometres (3 miles) north of Brisbane's city centre, and as the trees and gardens effectively form an extension of an adjoining bushland park, the tower does appear as a lookout or observation post. And of course, it being a tower means that it occupies far less of its site than a bungalow or villa. It was an environmentally deferential design, and the structure has inevitably and most compatibly provided a home for local wildlife: possums, bats, birds, insects and the ubiquitous bush turkeys.

The interior of the house is just as memorable as the exterior, but not so much for its response to climate and ecology, and its utilization of polygonal geometry, as for its application of a curiously conservative sumptuousness. The elemental external assemblage, the 'timber and tin', conceals an almost baronial, certainly High Victorian residence, wherein a sequence of staircases with ornately carved balustrades sweep up through five levels of dark timber-walled rooms illuminated through stained-glass windows. It is as though Hall and his sister amalgamated two types of nineteenth-century Australian architecture to erect a house that was frugal yet plush, and austere yet accommodating, thus averting a stylistic conflict inherent to modernism, which has rarely found a satisfactory method to accommodate the accrued comforts of history within its orthogonal measure.

ABOVE AND OPPOSITE The interiors are richly crafted and ornamented in a pre-modernist, almost late-nineteenth-century fashion.

ADDISON HOUSE

1999
BRISBANE, AUSTRALIA
REX ADDISON

The house that Rex Addison designed for himself and his wife Susan on the tangled bushy slopes of a gully in inner-west Brisbane was a statement of singularity, born from an allegiance to conformity. Addison is the quintessential Queenslander, and, pardon the pun, so was his house (typologically speaking, a 'Queenslander' is a house native to the Brisbane region, typified by broad verandahs, wide eaves and its elevation above the ground). After training at the University of Queensland and the Architectural Association in London, Addison set up practice in Brisbane in the early 1970s, where he quickly emerged as a seminal figure in what must now be acknowledged as a uniquely gifted and committed generation of architects. That generation did not form a movement, or even mutually agree on a style or direction (a typically Queensland characteristic, you might say), but their legacy is cohesive and formidable. Addison and his peers[1] responded directly to the climate, topography and landscape of their subtropical region, and their works can be pinpointed as one of the first genuine manifestations of an architecture that is now referred to as sustainable and environmentally aware.

Addison's first widely publicized project was the home for his young family, built in 1975 on a thickly vegetated Brisbane hillside. The design could be viewed, as it most certainly was by Addison himself, as a reinstatement of the traditional, intrinsically sustainable Queenslander house, and considering the not-very-tropicalized modernism that had prevailed for many decades, that was indeed a groundbreaking event. For several years in the late 1970s, Addison lived and worked in Papua New Guinea (PNG), where he honed his approach to the fundamentals of tropical design and construction, and his subsequent career was notable for a collection of houses and small public buildings with a very individual, very identifiable expression. An aesthetic reverence for local Brisbane characteristics and subtropical vernacular was fused with forms and spatial patterns derived from the Arts and Crafts, and Frank Lloyd Wright in particular. Addison then took a step back from his career to rethink his life and apply his energies to the construction of his new home and studio on a large plot of land he had inherited from his parents in suburban Taringa.

Erudite, knowledgeable and well-versed in all things beyond architecture, Addison was a man who had seen the world, yet rather like Henry David Thoreau at Walden, he decided to 'live deliberately' and to 'live deep' in

OPPOSITE The east elevation of the house comprises an assemblage of lightweight materials, with panels that serve as sheltering overhangs and translucent walls. **ABOVE** The living and dining areas are embraced by the tropical garden. Rex Addison designed all the furniture and fittings.

a place of his own choosing: Thoreau escaped to the woods, and Addison retreated to the backyard of his childhood home. He sold off the street-facing bungalow and its lawns and kept the remainder as the site for a wonderfully immersive and introspective compound, which was imbued in all its forms and details by references that were both autobiographical and allegorical. At the bottom of the gully, the studio was built first, and it was appreciated and publicized as a stand-alone project, one that Addison refers to twenty-five years later as: 'Maybe my best effort...I certainly feel the working drawing (on one sheet) was my best.' It was a little gem, perched on low stumps above a dry creek bed as a rigorously composed almost-symmetrical pavilion with an exposed timber framework and a dramatically pitched roof form. The house was completed a year later, stepping down the hillside at right angles to the studio, with which it formed an elongated C-shaped site plan enclosing stands of trees and clumps of ferns. As with the studio, the architecture was sharply delineated and the tectonic ordering, the combination of materials, was comforting and homely. Both the external forms and the internal spaces were richly embroidered and comprised nothing less than a homage to Addison himself, as quixotic artist as much as disciplined architect. For example, the poles beneath the house were stained red to remind him of chewed betel nut residue in PNG, and the sliding plywood skylight panels – operated by pulleys weighed with great balls of lead shot – have a palm-frond motif inscribed by Addison.

In its programmatic scope and its charmingly idiosyncratic expression, Addison House was a remarkable exercise in architectural commitment, one that could not have been realized without a creative restlessness on the one hand, and a deep respect for place and tradition on the other. In all its details and tangents, the architecture was experimental, yet it was empirically derived. As with his previous family home, it was a critical reinterpretation of a localized tropical form (the 'Queenslander'), and in the light-filled expansiveness of its spatial and material awareness, it must be seen as a prototype for enlightened, environmentally attuned architecture everywhere. It was not exclusively tropical.

ABOVE Sliding plywood skylights in the living areas are inscribed with a palm-frond motif and operated by pulleys weighed down with lead shot.

ABOVE A large timber balcony rises high above the gardens and the studio.

ABOVE The almost symmetrical structure of the studio is raised above a dry creek bed at the bottom of the garden.

TOP The studio has an 'exaggerated' expressionist quality, clearly referencing the forms of the tropical vernacular. Rex Addison can be seen at the entry.

PRECIMA AND SCHNYDER HOUSES

1989 and 1991
KUALA LUMPUR, MALAYSIA
JIMMY LIM

'Tropical architecture wasn't really in my head...it was in my being. I had grown up in it. I had absorbed everything,' says Jimmy Lim. Lim grew up in Penang, in a Chinese kampong[1] house built by his grandfather, which was essentially an open structure with very few partitions. As he remembers, 'We didn't even have fans, never mind air-conditioning. Our house was only cooled through open windows.' And Lim loved it. He loved the ambience, he loved the family and community lifestyle, and he was already fascinated by timber construction and the variety of styles displayed throughout the kampong. He went on to study architecture in Sydney at the University of New South Wales, where he quickly revealed his true inclinations by submitting a proposal for an elevated timber structure with a pitched roof for his second-year design assignment. He received a 'fail', but he was not deterred, and, as he recalls, by his third year he had moved up from 'fail' to 'questionable'. He graduated in 1968 and worked for several years in Sydney before returning to Malaysia in 1972, where he learnt the ropes at a large firm in Kuala Lumpur and set up his own practice in 1978. His first completed project was a house on the site of an old rubber plantation. As the structure was built from timber[2] and as it was clearly not 'modernist', it attracted much attention and received an award from PAM (the Malaysian Institute of Architects). From here on, for a period of roughly fifteen years, the story of Jimmy Lim mirrors the story of tropical architecture in Southeast Asia, especially at the level of the private house.

On his return to Malaysia, Lim had assiduously studied traditional architecture and construction, and when he began his own practice, he immediately incorporated his own research and development 'department'. This took the form of an ever-evolving structure-cum-house, where he could experiment to his heart's content: 'I tried all my ideas there, nobody else

OPPOSITE AND ABOVE The interiors of the Schnyder House display Jimmy Lim's highly detailed structural virtuosity. A double-height living room is adjoined by a low-ceilinged dining area.

ABOVE Decorated with the owners' artefacts, the bedroom and bathroom in the Schnyder House are dark and shuttered.

wanted to be first with innovations.' In the early 1980s, Lim was pretty much out on his own, and when asked to recall anybody else who was doing work that even looked tropical (and what we would now describe as sustainable), he is bemused by the memories:

> There was none of this going on at all. The only references I had were the books by Maxwell Fry and Jane Drew. I read them, but the work was set in Nairobi, and it didn't relate because of the high altitude. Here in Malaysia, it's the humidity that knocks you down. So you must have air movement, you need architecture without walls, but you also need protection from rain, so you need walls that can float away! I experimented with everything – with openings, with large overhangs – and I was the first to do away with gutters, because they are always clogged with leaves. I was way ahead of my time. It wasn't called sustainable back then, I was simply being efficient and frugal. I was using passive energy for comfort, and I was always looking at the old kampong houses, picking up all the tricks – how they maintained the wood, how the windows were operated, how the air was circulated. My architecture was expressive, but that was simply a manifestation of its functionality. And right from the start, I did not want to disturb the natural environment.

Set in adjacency on a low ridge in Bangsar, a suburb of Kuala Lumpur, the Precima House was completed in 1989 and the Schnyder House in 1991. They were ostensibly built as separate dwellings – with a different style and plan – for the two partners of a Swiss watch company. With the passing of time and the permutations of various domestic arrangements, the houses have effectively merged and become one, and as such represent a resplendent and still-intact museum for the architecture of Jimmy Lim. The Precima House has a reinforced concrete framework, which Lim concedes was a 'compromise', while the two bedroom pavilions flanking the pool were built from wood. The soaring volume of the house is a sight to behold, a wonderful light-filled atrium ornamented in profusion by extensive timber bracketing, which Lim appropriated from traditional Chinese architecture; as he says, 'I innovated to produce junctions as an integrated structural system, and I was clamping double beams. I didn't want to use a single beam that would span a great distance.'

Schnyder House has a timber framework, with an external form derived from the traditional architecture of Sarawak in Borneo. As with the earlier house, the interior spaces comprised another exposition of Lim's highly detailed structural virtuosity, rising over two levels above a pool terrace that extends as an open cloister across the ground floor. A low-ceilinged dining area opens out into a double-height living room, and – wrapped, clad and enveloped by dark-stained woodwork – the entire space has an unmistakably ecclesiastical air, which was, somewhat amusingly, the architect's intention: 'I have always thought that if you consider that a temple is the house of God, then a house should be a temple to yourself.'

ABOVE The exterior form of the Schnyder House is derived from the traditional architecture of Sarawak.

OPPOSITE The central volume of the Precima House contains a soaring atrium with a dark-stained timber structural support system.

ABOVE The structure of the Precima House features a bracketing system of clamped double beams, which Jimmy Lim appropriated from traditional Chinese architecture.

ABOVE View from the entry of the Precima House, looking across the atrium to the bedroom wings.

BAWA, BALI AND THE TROPICAL RESORT

'The significance of Bawa's work lies in the act of raising both the formal and popular Indigenous traditions from the degraded status assigned to them in the colonial era, and in the creation from them of a formal architectural language.'
SHANTI JAYAWARDENE[1]

The legacy of Geoffrey Bawa is intriguing and somewhat paradoxical, if not contradictory. He studied law at the University of Cambridge and practised as a barrister in London, before returning to his homeland of Sri Lanka after the Second World War to work for a Colombo law firm, whereupon he purchased an abandoned rubber plantation at Lunuganga in 1948 with the intention of renovating the existing bungalow as a sumptuous villa surrounded by a tropicalized Italianate garden. Chagrined by his lack of expertise for such a task, he headed back to the UK and trained at the much-esteemed Architectural Association in London, graduating in 1957 and returning once again to Sri Lanka in the following year. He quickly proved to be quite an architect, continuing in practice for some forty years, and his projects were notable for their gentle and graceful sensitivity, their evocation of a tropical languor and their quiet yet insistent championing of local craft. As Shanti Jayawardene contends: 'The significance of Bawa's work lies in the act of raising both the formal and popular Indigenous traditions from the degraded status assigned to them in the colonial era, and in the creation from them of a formal architectural language.'[2] Many commentators have, however, observed that he was quite content to perpetuate the idyll of the colonial lifestyle and the indulgences of the elite; as Anoma Pieris remarks: 'He romanticized the scenographic possibilities of the tropical landscape, and revived the colonial habits of leisure concomitant with their appreciation.'[3] The sociopolitical implications of Bawa's cultural and historical cross-referencing continue to permeate architectural expression across a region where the attainment of national independence, economic security and societal integration had been (and occasionally remains) problematic.

Bawa straddled two divides, which were in essence a reflection of the realities and uncertainties of post-war Asia. The first was social as well as aesthetic: the colonial (entrenched and avaricious) was giving way to the post-colonial (as yet unformed and in search of identity), and it was the act of the served handing over to the servant. The second set his modernist training against his love for the craft of the vernacular. As Pieris points out, he certainly resolved these issues in a 'scenographic' sense, yet he also did so, crucially, in a typological sense. His range of houses, many of which were conversions, established a universally acceptable image of tasteful tropicality that may forever prevail, as will, in a more formal outcome, his deft arrangement of internal courtyards as devices for providing daylight and stimulating cross-ventilation.

His masterwork was the great estate at Lunuganga, a touchstone for cross-cultural 'scenography', yet his most quantifiable legacy was to be found in the field of hotel design, where his achievements had an immediate impact across the region, and, ipso facto, on the emergence of the tropical house. Before Bawa designed the Bentota Beach Hotel in 1967, resort architecture in Asia (not that there was much) had little in the way of genius loci – the spirit of the place. Bawa's design for a very large hotel south of Colombo was resolutely modern, as indeed it had to be for its anticipated marketplace, but it was also comprehensively imbued with tropicality, in all its natural and delightful guises.

Nowhere was the significance and effectiveness of Bawa's 'tropical modernist' resort parti acknowledged more keenly than in Bali, where despair and outrage had followed the erection of the Bali Beach Hotel in 1966, a multi-storeyed modernist intrusion upon a beatified landscape. After that, it could be said that the design of nearly every Balinese resort deferred to Bawa's template, as would a plethora of tropical house designs, to the point (some thirty years later) where architects in Malaysia and Singapore would refer derisively to the generic exotica of a Bali style: pitched tile roofs, gently bubbling water courses, deftly placed Indigenous artefacts, frangipanis, wind chimes, and so on.

As it happened, Bawa himself was instrumental in determining the course of Balinese architecture in a much more personal fashion. In 1973, he was asked by Australian painter Donald Friend – a very well-travelled, larger-than-life character, and an inveterate and somewhat notorious socialite[4] – to assist with his development of the Batujimbar estate at Sanur, on the island's eastern beachfront. Bawa's house and museum for Friend, built in 1974, was a lovingly and perfectly composed piece of reverential architecture, one which borrowed judiciously from the timeless forms and proportions of Bali's water-garden palaces. For a few short years, Friend's compound at Batujimbar

ABOVE The original bungalow in the grounds of Lunuganga, Bentota, Sri Lanka.

ABOVE Geoffrey Bawa, Batujimbar House and Museum, Bali, Indonesia, 1974.

served as the scene for architectural exchanges that would have far-reaching influence. In 1970, Friend invited the Sydney-based architect Peter Muller to stay at Batujimbar, and he duly became fascinated by Bali (and subsequently by Bawa), as did another frequent visitor, Kerry Hill, a young Australian who had been engaged as the site architect for the nearby Bali Hyatt and would go on to make quite a name for himself.

Muller was best known for a series of 'Wrightian' houses built in Sydney's bushland suburbs during the 1950s, and, shortly after his arrival in Bali, he would be responsible for a breakthrough that rivalled that of Bawa in Bentota. He had been asked to design a beachfront house for an American acquaintance at Jimbaran, but the project grew and, by the time construction began in late 1973, it had somehow morphed into a seventy-five room resort hotel. Taking a step sideways from tropical modernism, Muller was adamant that the design should comprise an uninflected (untainted) rendition of traditional Balinese architecture, built and crafted only by local tradesmen. The architecture for the hotel (eventually named the Bali Oberoi) was tropical vernacular, and the hand of a Westerner with a modernist training was hard to detect, certainly in a tectonic sense. Muller went on to design the quintessential Balinese resort with the Aman Dari in 1988, and the influence that his insistence upon vernacular purity has had on the region's architecture – and the course of house design in particular – cannot be overestimated.

ABOVE Peter Muller, Bali Oberoi Hotel, Bali, Indonesia, 1978.

ABOVE Peter Muller, Aman Dari Resort, Bali, Indonesia, 1988.

SAMUJANA

2014
KOH SAMUI, THAILAND
GFAB ARCHITECTS

Gary Fell has a very clear idea of how he wants to design in the tropics. A graduate of the Bartlett School of Architecture in London, he worked for two years as site architect for John Heah's Four Seasons Sayan resort in Bali and remained on the island to set up his own practice, Gfab, in 1999. The Four Seasons was a bit of a game-changer for Balinese resort architecture, denoting a shift from vernacular homage to interpretation and representation, and, in terms of its formal language, it could be seen as a tribute (not a pastiche) to mid-twentieth-century modernism, that of John Lautner in particular. Scenographically, the imposition of structurally expressive architecture on the forested slopes of Balinese gorges was a good fit – the vision of cleanly sculpted quasi-heroic forms emerging from the palm trees had a most agreeable panache. Fell's architecture has not deviated from this template, although in the interests of his own 'purist' outlook, he has foresworn the use of the curved line. When asked to point to the major influences on his work, he replies: 'The obvious one is Neutra. He is the godfather of setting up that inside/outside relationship. And I am a great fan of Niemeyer.' To reduce that to base essentials, Fell has taken heed of Richard Neutra's strategies for open planning and added the formal flair of Oscar Niemeyer – all his houses are essays on the invisibility of the inside/outside boundary, and they are sculpturally defined by a bright-white geometric framework.

The Samujana project was, for somebody with Fell's inclinations, a dream commission. The scrubby and rocky site was located on a headland at the northeast tip of Koh Samui, and fabulous views over the sea and the mountainous landscape could be had from all points on the slope. The first villa was built in 2004, with another 27 completed as holiday houses for individual clients by 2014. The initial concept – the proportions, the geometries, the materials, the expression – did not waver, but it was adapted to the particularity of each context. The architecture was comprised of variations on a theme, as Fell explains:

> The designs were essentially the same, but each villa had a unique layout, responding to the specific topography. I simply wasn't able to repeat any design. The site was littered with large rock outcrops, and they were integrated into each house as 'features'. The sloping site

LEFT As an integrated composition, the villas and landscaping cascade down the hillside to the sea.

meant that most of the villas were entered at the highest point, and the descent followed the natural terrain.

The villas have a wonderful sense of spaciousness and expansiveness. In the balmy tropical maritime climate, an ambience of languor is exacerbated by the framing of the panoramas as an infinite vista. Fell is at pains to point out that as the designs placed such emphasis upon space, luxury can be realized without recourse to expensive materials, and that the program was innately sustainable: 'The houses make extensive use of passive cooling methods to save energy. Pools and gardens are used for roofs; huge overhangs and massive stone walls keep the building cool; and atria with reflecting pools encourage breezes and cross-ventilation.' The capacious living areas are open to the elements, occasionally walled by sandstone excavated on site, or by existing rock formations, and a tectonic juxtaposition between the organic and the cleanly orthogonal is calibrated at every turn. The shaping of form, both in plan and section, is perhaps the most captivating aspect of the architecture – the layering and terracing have an integrated right-angled geometry that works its way over the entire site, down to the sea between the rocks and through the palm trees.

ABOVE The architecture for each of the villas demonstrates Gary Fell's delight in the material expression of mid-twentieth-century modernism.

ABOVE Strategies for passive cooling are used throughout, with huge overhangs, thick stone walls and extensive breezeways.

ABOVE AND OVERLEAF From the open-plan open-air living areas, the panoramas of the sea and mountains are framed as an infinite vista.

ABOVE Mist rises from an entry pond, which continues as a watercourse that runs through the length of the house.

BEA HOUSE

2008
JAKARTA, INDONESIA
STUDIO TONTON

Located in a residential estate some 20 kilometres (12 miles) west of central Jakarta, Bea House is a hidden gem, a meticulously detailed and beautifully proportioned exercise in living, breathing tropical design with a Scandi-Japanese twist. The single-storey villa is discreetly tucked away behind an enveloping screen of trees, and the very wide spread of a low-pitched roof is all that can be glimpsed over the entry gardens. The structure is simple, that of a very refined hut built with a steel frame on a rectangular plan. Two sets of rooms – 'servant and served' spaces – flank a central spine, a promenade that unfolds from west to east as a quite remarkable sequence of interior design configurations. Although the house is small, every composition and every detail has been treated with the utmost finesse, as if it were a high-end tropical resort – the regional typology for which Studio TonTon, the locally based partnership of Antony Liu and Ferry Ridwan, is best known.

The elegantly battened timber soffits of the entry are extended over the central corridor and through each of the rooms, which are illuminated by daylight softened by layers of translucent polycarbonate. All the volumes and all the spaces have an interconnected system of natural ventilation, whereby air flows without impediment through wide openings and slender vertical screens. Made from the wood of the bangkirai tree, the strips of timber battening also clad the corridor's walls and the screens in the public and entry areas, and every space is furnished with a carefully crafted ambience not often encountered in the tropics. The

ABOVE The entry lobby is roofed and screened by timber battens and a galvanized-steel framework.

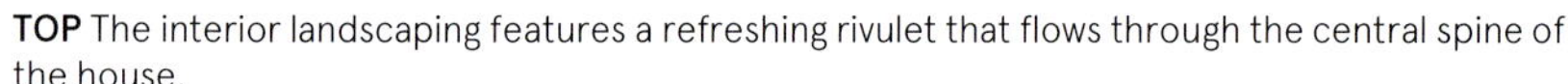

TOP The interior landscaping features a refreshing rivulet that flows through the central spine of the house.

ABOVE Opening out to private courtyards, the bedrooms have a finely detailed resort-style elegance.

bedrooms, on the southern side of the corridor, are entered through 'secret' doorways invisible to the naked eye, camouflaged by the repetitive rhythms of the slatted timber wall. The master bedroom opens out to a private courtyard with minimalist Zen-like landscaping, and that sense of artful composition and material richness was also applied to the interior design of each room. As with a certain type of resort, most notably those designed by Kerry Hill, the cumulative weight of such finely detailed elegance is ultimately measured in degrees of sumptuousness – or sustainable luxury, as some proponents would have it.

The real joy of the architecture, however, is in the interior landscaping. As Liu and Ridwan recall: 'When we were first looking at the site, it was evening, and a mist was rising over the nearby lake. It was a magical moment. We were struck by the idea that we could "bring this moment" to the architecture. We wanted to unlock the separation between the natural world and the mass of the building.' What they brought to the architecture was a rivulet that runs the length of the house, through the central spine as an internal stream, separated from the corridor by a glass wall braced by columns of galvanized steel. The watercourse actually begins in the forecourt, where clouds of mist appear to be rising from a pond and the adjoining beds of stone. The mist is artificially induced, and the process extends throughout the house, both as a delightful 'natural' feature, and as a method for cooling, which succeeds in reducing the temperature by as much as 3°C. Thunbergia vines planted at the western entry have spread to the east, over the riverbed, to serve as a drooping layer of natural insulation and environmental mediation, which operates in conjunction with the stands of bamboo that screen the service zones to the north. Over a pebbled bed lined by granite boulders, the rivulet flows serenely through the heart of the house as part of an internal landscape that is not just a garden, but a parkland.

TOP The bedrooms are entered through 'secret' doorways (left), while the service areas (right) are hidden behind vines. **ABOVE** The landscaping of the master bedroom courtyard has a minimal Japanese aesthetic.

WALL HOUSE

2000
AUROVILLE, INDIA
ANUPAMA KUNDOO ARCHITECTS

As most of the economies of tropical Asia grew steadily more buoyant in the late twentieth century, the validity of the area's architecture was framed by a discourse that Anoma Pieris describes as 'a regionalist debate where rapid globalization posed a threat to national cultures derived from the rural vernacular.' She goes on to make the salient point that: 'In Southeast Asia, urbanization and affluence was relegating the vernacular to remote rural communities and urban poor, unlike South Asia [India and Sri Lanka], where the vernacular was part of the everyday landscape.'[1] The sheer size of India in particular, and the socialist policies deployed by its post-independence governments, meant that construction in general retained a humble and inexpensive (Gandhi-esque) disposition, and the most interesting architecture could be seen as an assertion of localized community-minded identity. In South Asia, the utilization of vernacular forms and methods was not the re-creation of sustainable styles and methods, but a process of adaptation and innovation.

Auroville – an ashram, commune and planned township – was the creation of 'The Mother', Mirra Alfassa, the French-born spiritual partner and devotee of Sri Aurobindo, with whom she had founded the now universally revered ashram in Pondicherry in the early 1920s. The Mother had long idealized a settlement that would transcend national borders and human division, and when the notion was ratified by the Indian government (and commended by UNESCO), work began on a site five miles north of Pondicherry in 1968. Although the plan was primarily devised by French architect Roger Anger as a collection of demarcated zones within a nuclear (cosmic) ring, Auroville took its essential character from its wonderfully porous assimilation with the existing landscape and villages. Quite the opposite of a gated community (as per most Indian facilities for spiritual guidance), Auroville was open to all, with residents who had foresworn selfishness in favour of a collective economy, and who were as indentured to the immediate land and resources as the neighbouring villagers.

An extremely distinctive style of architecture then came into being on the dry plains of the Coromandel Coast. The rich red earth had always been used to make bricks, pots and tiles, and in the hands of the architects of Auroville, the bricks were used abundantly to create dwellings and community buildings with unexpectedly quirky formal dispositions. In keeping with the make-up of the community, the architecture reflected both Indian and Western sources,

OPPOSITE View from the south, looking to the lofty vaulted loggia that centres the house.

ABOVE A bedroom projects as an alcove from a wall of red brick on the eastern elevation.

OPPOSITE The catenary roof of the vaulted loggia is built with curving tubes made from clay pots.

and if pushed to define a style, one might suggest a 'brick brutalism' adapted from the formal gestures of Le Corbusier, Oscar Niemeyer and Balkrishna Doshi, with overriding geometries occasionally rendered in concrete.

Located in Auroville's 'research and experimentation' zone, Wall House was formulated by Anupama Kundoo as a comely synthesis of modernist architectural rigour and overtly vernacularized construction. Built from local bricks, timber and stone, the genius loci of the structure was unquestionably in place, and it was intrinsically sustainable – the unrelieved massing, erect forms and voluminous openings of the structure read as a diagram for designing in response to the microclimate and orientation of the site. Yet the architecture was imbued with something much more – it was beguiling and it was heroic. The house was not large, but it was centred around and defined by a great vaulted space, a loggia with a classical proportion and an artfully crafted interior, and as Kundoo states: 'The spatial concept pays homage to the early modernist architects who put forth the ideas of "open plan" architecture for homes.' The monumental catenary roof was formed of curving tubes made from clay pots, as were smaller vaults, and both the system and the resultant expression paid a further homage to modernism, in this case Le Corbusier's Maisons Jaoul (1954–56), where brick spans were used as moulds for concrete and exposed as arched ceilings throughout the interior.

Completed at the turn of the millennium, Wall House was an especially timely exercise in demonstrating the virtues of conflating environmental control with architectonic creativity, and it received quite a degree of international attention (for example, a same-size facsimile was constructed for the 2012 Architectural Biennale in Venice). Oddly enough, however, in light of both Auroville's spiritual aspirations and India's post-independence affirmations of social equity, it is clear that Kundoo's architecture was born of pragmatism – motivated by program, by placement and process rather than by symbolism and cultural/contextual relationships.

OPPOSITE AND ABOVE The interiors display a synthesis of modernist architectural rigour and vernacular construction techniques.

HARDY HOUSE

1997

SAYAN, BALI, INDONESIA

CHEONG YEW KUAN

Malaysia-born and Singapore-trained Cheong Yew Kuan would go on to have an illustrious career, designing resorts and fantasy-isle getaways for the rich and famous, but it is fair to say that none of his works had quite the immediate, visceral impact of Hardy House, an avowedly rustic tree house in Bali and his earliest project. Kuan moved from Singapore to Bali in 1994, when he set up practice in order to assume control of a hotel project he had been working on as a graduate in Kerry Hill's office. That commission, the exclusive Begawan Giri resort, was completed in 1999 to great acclaim, acknowledged as one of the most individual and accomplished of the then-proliferating reinterpretations of traditional Balinese architecture. Kuan then chose to veer away from the appropriation of traditional iconography and apply himself to the development of a contemporary architecture that had contextual and cultural integrity. In retrospect, the Hardy House – located on a level site high above the plunging slopes of the Ayung River gorge – might thus be considered as something of an anomaly, acquiescing in spirit and ambience to a rather hackneyed vision of Bali as a paradise without compare, but, in fact, it did not look Balinese. In terms of its proportion, structure and ornamentation, the closest similarity would be that of the *penghulu* (headman) house still seen in Malay villages – rigorously assembled with post-and-lintel structures raised on stilts and screened and ventilated by decorative shutters. As with colonial adaptations of that typology, Kuan transformed the sheltered, but essentially residual ground-floor space into a lofty living and entertainment area.

The appearance is primal, and the linear structure could be mistaken on first glimpse, through the trees in silhouette, for an elevated longhouse built in a rudimentary fashion, but closer inspection reveals the tight ordering logic of the post-and-beam framework. Forked tree trunks in the living space are used as props, both for structural bracing and for theatrical suggestion, as

OPPOSITE AND ABOVE Viewed from the east, high above the Ayung River gorge, the house has an open living area surmounted by a screened and shuttered layer of bedrooms.

symbols of primitive construction. The siting was also quite theatrical, with the house sitting on an island within a shallow pool, as if a great timber boat or ark – an allusion that was singularly appropriate for the true performative role of the house. Commissioned by jewelers John and Cynthia Hardy, who have resided in Bali since 1975 and most famously founded the Green School in 2008, the house was not just a dwelling – it was a gathering place, showroom and gallery with a tropicalized Arts and Crafts expression. As seen in his subsequent high-end commissions, Kuan was not just an architect, he was an interior designer with a special fascination for furniture, and in a somewhat ironic counterpoint to the intrinsically primitive appearance of its construction, the decor of Hardy House is unreservedly luxuriant.

Hardy House was a one-liner and a one-off, and although it was widely publicized, it did not lead to any tangible progressions or variations, and any hint of homage was effectively to vernacular architecture as much as Kuan's interpretation thereof. It should not however, be regarded as a folly, as such declaredly outré pieces of architecture usually are. There was a very pragmatic rationale that underpinned the structural framework, and the spatial arrangement in particular. The structural components, the living spaces, the immediate landscape and the superstructure of the bedroom volume, were all accorded an individual expression of their purpose, yet they were each subservient to an overall harmony and the beauty of the environment. The design was elemental, sumptuous and perfectly resolved, and, as might be quietly remarked on in conversation, it does seem that the smallest (and earliest) projects by an eminent architect are often the most beautifully composed.

ABOVE AND RIGHT The post-and-beam framework is supplemented by props made from forked tree trunks.

LUNUGANGA

1948–2003
BENTOTA, SRI LANKA
GEOFFREY BAWA

In the late 1940s, Geoffrey Bawa relinquished his position with a Colombo law practice and set off for two years' travel around the world. The son of a prominent lawyer, he was well-off, and he made overtures to buy a villa overlooking Lake Garda, but upon return to Sri Lanka in 1948, he decided to purchase an abandoned rubber estate 60 kilometres (40 miles) south of Colombo. His intentions were clear – he wished to create his own ornamental landscape, a set of pleasure gardens with Dedduwa Lake as an idyllic backdrop. And he would train as an architect to do so.[1] Until his death in 2003, Bawa continued to work on his landscape – to add and subtract, both as an architect and a gardener – and as his fame and reputation grew, so did those of his estate, and the very name 'Lunuganga' became synonymous with the vision of a cultivated tropical arcadia.

Bawa was reputedly at pains to point out that at Lunuganga the architecture was not important, it was all about the landscape, but that was an expression of diffidence and ingenuousness – he could hardly engage in a process of non-design. In essence, and this is critical to understanding the significance of Lunuganga, the buildings were designed, or pieced together,

OPPOSITE Sculptures and artefacts are artfully placed throughout the grounds, drawing on the traditions of romantic European gardens.

ABOVE The lowest lakeside terrace was envisaged as part of a tropicalized pleasure garden, composed with a European inflection.

TOP Built in a contemporary modernist style, a sloping set of studios has acquired a patina of agelessness and gently merges with the jungle.

ABOVE A small Italianate loggia serves as a gateway and teahouse in the terraced landscape above the lake.

as objects within a picturesque landscape, as carefully considered parts of that landscape. Bawa was, of course, drawing upon the traditions of the great European gardens, and specifically the romantic English landscapes of the eighteenth century, but he was doing so in a tropical wilderness, and the precepts underwent a form of transmutation – artfulness was replaced with a knowing artlessness. Trees and plants grew so quickly that vistas might change within a week, and the process of weathering was so immediate and endemic that the appearance of the buildings was unalterably entropic – they were discolouring and wearing away as soon as they were erected. And this was to Bawa's liking; it meant that he could (unlike Capability Brown, William Kent and Humphrey Repton) devise a landscape for his own pleasure that was almost instantly 'historicized'.

For all its grand aspirations, Lunuganga was, from the moment of its inception, planned to serve as a home for Bawa's extensive network of friends and family, for members of his architectural practice and for a retinue of international visitors and guests. The process began with the piecemeal adaptation of an existing rundown bungalow, which was perfectly poised on the crest of the site's northernmost hill, looking from high over the lake and the verdant, seemingly untouched countryside. With subtle stylistic and structural adjustments, Bawa played up the neoclassical, Italianate appearance of the British colonial typology, and that 'look' became the underlying aesthetic for all subsequent construction and/or alterations. New buildings were built sporadically over the next fifty years, with several – such as the guest pavilions secluded on the southern extremity of the grounds – featuring strictly proportioned Palladian façade. Small loggias and rustic workers' sheds were dotted as follies throughout the landscape, and as with all the buildings, the vegetation was encouraged to intrude and integrate. In this quasi-historical context, such an artless merging of trees and masonry can be appreciated as a form of tropical architectural language – as derived from the ruins of Angkor Wat.

In its scope and ambition, Lunuganga formed a tableau, and it was one that portrayed a romanticized

ABOVE The guesthouse pavilions at the south of the grounds display a delightfully erudite Palladian sense of proportion.

post-colonial image of Sri Lanka. To an extent, that vision was shared by other singular artistic talents of a generation that had lived through the last days of the country as a colony, but Bawa was an architect and landscaper, not a sculptor, painter or fabric designer. His masterwork thus constitutes a more literal – and possibly more wistful – reiteration of times gone by, and it was an indubitable expression of his own personal taste. Lunuganga served as a destination and rendezvous for the cultured and the worldly, and it might be suggested that it was something of a Sri Lanka for foreigners – one where the vernacular had a colonial twist, and the vistas had a European directive.

Unless one refers to the myriad details – the oversized pyramid that roofs the henhouse, or the couchant reshaping of the iconic frangipani on the northern lawn – the direct influence of Lunuganga is difficult to quantify. With his re-application of the traditional courtyard house as a substitute for the bungalow type on tight urban sites, and with his very timely 'invention' of the 'tropical modern' resort hotel (at nearby Bentota Beach), Bawa had a more than significant impact on the recent typological history of architecture. Yet in the greater scheme of things, the legacy of Lunuganga resides more in the creation of a spirit of place, an achievement made possible by the deferential subjugation of his personal inclinations and romantic imaginings to the performative processes of the natural environment.

ABOVE View from the north over the swathe of sweeping lawns laid out by Bawa as a corridor through the jungle.

ABOVE Geoffrey Bawa cultivated, and deliberately reshaped, a low-spreading frangipani that frames the view from the bungalow over Dedduwa Lake.

MALALASEKERA HOUSE

2011
COLOMBO, SRI LANKA
C. ANJALENDRAN

The houses of C. Anjalendran represent a fundamental, almost unequivocal, distillation of an architectural parti that provides a clean and clear framework for all manner of extraneous and eclectic expression. As Anjalendran says, 'I do not like decorative architecture. I expose the structure as far as possible, and I do not cheat. A house should display the lives of the occupants, not the architects.' To that end, he deploys a trabeated (not arched and devoid of curves) system of exposed concrete columns and beams. That framework stands stark and unadorned, in plain sight yet somehow unseen, receding in deference to gardens, paintings, furniture, fabrics and sculptures, all of which form part of a distinctively Sri Lankan way of living and decorating. Emanating from Colombo, a beguiling and somewhat mysterious artistic sensibility has fascinated purveyors of style (and architects) across the region and beyond for several decades, and Anjalendran – now well into his seventies – remains as its embodiment: 'I learnt from Geoffrey Bawa, Ena de Silva, Barbara Sansoni and Laki Senanayake.[1] I am first and foremost a proud Sri Lankan.'

The house for Swasha and Ashan Malalasekera and their family is located in a relatively sedate and leafy quarter of an increasingly hectic city, and it appears as little more than a yellow painted wall from the street. The outlook

OPPOSITE AND ABOVE Looking toward the house and its internal courtyard from the lawns and gardens on the east.

of the house is to the east, to a lushly planted garden centred by a stately mango tree, and Anjalendran says that the two levels of interiors, leading toward that landscape, were designed as a 'promenade of surprising spaces and diversity of experiences'. Both floors are primarily occupied by open-plan and open-sided living areas, meaning that the house is more or less defined by the accoutrements of its owners, and by the all-pervasive tropicality of the gardens, the tiled roofs and the sweeping timber ceilings. Slotted in-between the living areas and the rooms facing the street, a vertical courtyard serves as an abundantly vegetated reiteration of the rear garden, and the 'promenade of spaces' is made even more diverse by the absence of any discernible demarcation between inside and outside. And, of course, the house is brightly lit throughout, which Anjalendran explains in purely practical terms: 'Beneath the tropical sun, if the breadth of a house is more than thirty feet, it will be too dark to live. You need to have courtyards to provide daylight and cross-ventilation.'

Anjalendran may be insistent upon the provision of an architecturally blank canvas, but his creative hand is revealed in the treatment of those functional surfaces and components that do not serve to display the taste and lifestyle of the occupants. The pitched timber ceilings were built from light-toned lunumidella (mahogany), while the dark rafters were made from the wood of the nadum tree. Over the course of many years, having surveyed the ceilings of countless projects, Anjalendran settled upon a gap of 0.6 metres (2 feet) between the rafters (rather than the generally utilized 3 or 4 feet), which, as he notes, might appear to be an insignificant detail, but one that goes far in determining the look of a space. Occasional columns are crowned with ornate timber capitals, which are conspicuously oversized and overscaled as supports for concrete beams, and a colonnade leading to a guesthouse in the garden was devised as a gently composed and classically disposed piece of architecture in its own right, as was the lofty and courtly upstairs bathroom.

The overall impression of the Malalasekera House, especially as seen from the garden, is that of an uninflected, rather than idealized or romanticized, rendition of tropicality, and one that is very much a Sri Lankan phenomenon.[2] The landscape and climate of the island have conspired to produce an environment that is imbued with and pervaded by a luxuriant tropicality, and this attribute has long been celebrated – without exaggeration or embellishment – in its cultural and artistic representations. What Anjalendran is instinctively, and judiciously, drawing on and recreating is not so much the architecture that has gone before, but rather an abiding image of a tropical aesthetic and the invocation of arcadia.

ABOVE A colonnade leading to the guesthouse is gently scaled and classically disposed.

TOP An abundantly vegetated vertical courtyard between the two wings of the house provides daylight and cross-ventilation.

ABOVE Extending from the internal courtyard to the eastern gardens, the living and dining areas are open-plan and open-sided.

ABOVE A sculpture by Laki Senanayake is placed as a dividing screen between the dining and living areas.

ABOVE The central courtyard serves as a 'ventilation shaft', drawing breezes up and out from the living areas. **OPPOSITE** A lofty bathroom adjoining the master bedroom, seen in the light of the early morning sun.

VILLAGE HOUSE

2016
SURAT, INDIA
HIREN PATEL ARCHITECTS

On the rural outskirts of Surat, a thriving mercantile city on the coast of Gujarat, a compound conceived as a set of pavilions and pleasure gardens is reached by a quiet road that winds through a rustic landscape of small orchards and pastures. Having grown up in a small village, the wealthy diamond merchant who commissioned Hiren Patel to provide him with a personal estate asked a simple question: 'Why can't I have houses like those in the villages?' As Patel recalls, 'Like most architects, I was initially inclined toward showing a strong architectural expression on such a fabulous site, but I was easily swayed. Perhaps it was "anti-architecture", but we decided to build a village instead.' The resultant compound, Village House, reclines on the shores of the Tapti River as a harmonious integration of trees, gardens, sculptures, pavilions, villas and water courses, where the only hints of opulence and 'strong expression' come from ornamental eclecticism and scenographic surety.

Measuring some 17,500 square metres (188,400 square feet), the site was square and flat with extremely fertile soil, and in accordance with the precepts of *Vastu Shastra*, Patel devised a site plan as a grid with squares of 2.4 metres (8 feet), which he assessed to be the individual human space required within a compound of this scale. *Vastu Shastra* can be interpreted as 'the science of architecture', and its principles have underpinned Hindi construction of houses, temples, villages, towns and gardens for over 5,000 years. The overall square mandala (or site plan) comprises a grid of smaller squares, most commonly in multiples of nine (three by three), which is laid out in accordance with the spiritual, natural and human worlds. Cosmology is thus intertwined with earthly necessity.

Upon entry, the extent of the estate is only partially glimpsed from pathways enclosed by gardens and coloured stone walls, before it is revealed from a 'public plaza' sheltered by the soaring upturned eaves of a 'vernacular' ceremonial structure, built from timber with an inverted pyramid profile. An axial pathway leads across a lawn, and through gardens with lotus ponds, to the heart of the compound, where another timber structure takes the form of a *bale* – the pitched-roof open-sided rectangular pavilion used in traditional Balinese residential compounds. Patel

OPPOSITE AND ABOVE The compound is entered through a 'public plaza', surmounted by a broad timber roof with an inverted pyramid profile.

co-opted the *bale* simply because it works so well – as an inside/outside ceremonial space for a landscaped compound in a hot climate, it cannot be improved upon. It should be noted that the transplanting – not just to India but anywhere in the world – of an ostensibly Balinese building type is not a form of cross-cultural fusion or borrowing, but the universal acceptance of a fresh architectural language (and an update on the previously ubiquitous neoclassical styles of resorts and compounds such as this).

As prescribed, the architectural language is that of a village, but not as an abstracted interpretation of vernacular styles. Each of the villas has an uninflected re-creation of colour and form, and, as in a typical Gujarati village, each was built with plaster walls and pitched roofs of terracotta tiles. As Patel is keen to stress, 'The landscape was more important than the architecture,' and two zones of buildings – public and private – were grouped as clusters within that all-embracing landscape, so that both precincts have a village-like familiarity and sense of interconnection. The gardens were variegated, and the placement of the plantings appears random rather than rigid, yet they flow across the site as a continuous entity. The logic of the underlying grid ensures that there is no loss of control, and the landscaping effectively delineates the zones and public/private roles of the entire compound. As a unifying device, Patel introduced a geometric motif, in the shape of a square overlaid with a four-leaved clover, which could be used across the compound – in isolation as over-scaled windows, or in repetition as tiling patterns and jali screens. The rhythms of decorative reiteration, running through the landscape and over the *Vastu Shastra* grid, are continued within the villas as occasional pieces of elaborate joinery.

The compound serves as both a collection of houses for an extended family and as a regular venue for gatherings and parties with at least two-hundred guests. The scale and range of amenities might be those of a resort, but the ambience and pervading sense of intimacy are manifestly those of a village. The client wanted something grounded, a place that really made him feel at home, and as Patel remarks, 'I was enticed and intrigued by that sense of humility. In architectural terms, that implied a respect for context and for the way that people still want to live.'

RIGHT Set upon a site plan laid out on a *Vastu Shastra* grid, a Balinese-style *bale* lies at the heart of the compound as a ceremonial space.

OPPOSITE A jali screen made of timber blocks serves as a partition in the formal dining and entertainment areas.

TOP AND ABOVE Rhythms of repetition and vibrant splashes of colour are used throughout the exterior and interior architecture.

SINGAPORE AND THE DILEMMAS OF TROPICAL MODERNISM

'The clean lines and Cartesian forms that delineated the house from its tropical backdrop accentuated the suddenness with which modern citizens had been extracted from their kampong habitat. Unlike the textured and tactile softness of the traditional vernacular, Singapore's new "Tropical House" was characterized by its very estrangement from the land and the climate.' ANOMA PIERIS[1]

Having achieved outright independence in 1965, Singapore began the sprint to modernity well before its regional neighbours – Lee Kuan Yew, the first prime minister of the country, banking in a Confucian manner upon the will and the resolve of the populace – but that process eventually left its architects in a rather incongruous position. The island state had in its possession an array of well-trained and forward-thinking architects, many of whom had designed (often in collaboration) a series of public buildings and apartments whose quasi-monumental forms displayed a memorable juxtaposition of compositional innovation with programmatic ambition. Somewhat sadly, however, that brief appearance in the spotlight came to an end in 1975, when the all-powerful government more or less decreed that any landmark building should be designed by eminent foreigners: in with I.M. Pei and Kenzo Tange, and out with the likes of Alfred Wong, William Lim and Tay Kheng Soon. Not surprisingly, a malaise set in, as there were very few commissions to be had, certainly not of a scope that might attract attention. Unfortunately, and this may have been an admission of defeat, whenever they did get a chance to catch the eye, the results were generally devoid of spark, originality and local flavour – the Singaporeans were designing like they were foreigners.

It is significant to note that architectural practice in Singapore (beyond the now-customary role of subservience, i.e. sharpening pencils for the pedigreed visitors) was to an extent sustained by the design of resort hotels across the region, and, as a direct consequence of the breakthroughs by Geoffrey Bawa and Peter Muller, there was an upsurge of interest in contextually appropriate and environmentally aware design. This, however, was not reflected in the design of private houses, certainly during the 1980s, when as Anoma Pieris pithily observes, 'Singapore's new "Tropical House" was characterized by its very estrangement from the land and the climate'.[2] And yes, it does seem somewhat ludicrous to note in retrospect that the unabashedly modernist houses of this time were referred to as 'tropical' – they were not; they could have resided quite happily in Mannheim or Melbourne. More tangible and place-specific notions of tropicality began to filter through to domestic architecture in the 1990s – given legitimacy, as it were, by the allure of the widely publicized resorts in Bali, Thailand and Malaysia.

Kerry Hill (see p. 108) recounts that as a young architect he learnt at the feet of Bawa and Muller during their time in Bali in the 1970s (the three remained great friends and confidantes): 'The question in my mind was – as a foreign architect, how do you build here? Peter Muller and Geoffrey Bawa helped unlock some of the answers. Geoffrey's formal planning exudes a sense of calm, while Peter had a craft-based approach that deftly includes innovation.'[3] Hill began his immersion in tropical design as the site architect for the Bali Hyatt (1973), and then worked in Jakarta for several years before setting up practice in Singapore in 1978. He specialized in the design of hotels and resorts, and his skill as an orchestrator of space, massing and

ABOVE Kerry Hill Architects, Garlick Avenue House, Singapore, 2005.

ABOVE Ernesto Bedmar Architects, Eu House 1, Singapore, 1994.

proportion would have a profound influence on the course of architecture in the region, albeit in a characteristically understated way. His architecture was not overcomplicated, it was finessed and polished – he used scenographic effects, but never overindulged, and, much in the manner of Bawa, he picked and he chose from a variety of sources, and there was a monumental strength and an underlying classical sense of order to everything he did. He only designed a few houses in Singapore, and his two-storey Cluny Hill House (1998) formed a clean and clinical amalgam of robust (Balinese) massing at the ground level, surmounted by a bungalow-style open-plan living area. Hill was clearly referencing the nearby black-and-white houses built in the 1920s (he himself lived in a series of them throughout his years in Singapore), and in his customary imperturbable fashion, he placed the effectiveness of his architecture – and the concomitant provision of a very comfortable lifestyle – above any dilemmas of appropriation.

William Lim's Reuter House of 1990 was the first house with a hint of resort-style tropicality to be widely publicized, and, as with Hill's Cluny Hill House, the fundamental intention was to reinstall the spirit and style of the colonial bungalow. The architecture was rather hesitant and uncertain, with Lim hedging his bets, unwilling to stray too far from the sureties of conventional (European) massing and framework. Ernesto Bedmar (see p. 186), on the other hand, an Argentinian with a sparkling unrestrained delight in the sybaritic, launched himself wholeheartedly into renditions of the Bali style with two houses for Geoffrey Eu (1994 and 1997), and the House at Swiss Club Road (1997), whose poolside elevation formed a white-painted simulacrum of Bawa's Museum and House (1974) at Batujimbar. Bedmar was nothing if not astute and ambitious; he was soon to shake the style up, and effectively reinvented it as a prototype for luxury, one which quickly became the archetype for a certain class of extremely upmarket villas throughout tropical Asia.

The 1990s were an interesting decade for Singaporean house design, even though most of the architecture – in hindsight – appears to be quite tentative and cautious. It was always cleanly expressed and it was always modernist (no hint of the rough and ready, no Jimmy Lim, no Troppo). Environmental awareness was increasingly extolled as a key ingredient, and the influences – aesthetic as well as programmatic – fluctuated between high modernism (in the style of Gerrit Rietveld, no less) and the measured integration of both a regional vernacular and the local colonial-era heritage. The acts of homage to the colonial bungalow and the dissemination of the Bali style had been relatively straightforward to implement, and they could only be greeted with approval by the well-to-do, but – and this is critical – the considerably more nuanced process of adapting modernist forms to a tropical lifestyle appeared to be the only strategy that would be countenanced by a notably earnest new generation of architects. Singapore's now-flourishing economy had firmly established an affluent middle class, eager to demonstrate their material wealth (double meaning intended), and the commissions were flowing.

ABOVE Tay Kheng Soon, King Albert Park House, Singapore, 1994.

Tay Kheng Soon, a prominent member of the generation that had been 'exiled' by the government decree of 1975, designed one last house whose forms and lines were avowedly Cartesian (to quote Pieris), but here the architecture demonstrably engaged with the land and the climate. The King Albert Park House (1994) was a beautiful white-painted assemblage with layered eaves, segmented double-height windows, cavernous light-filled voids as living areas and luscious water gardens, but for some reason, the architecture was out of step. Perhaps it came too late – maybe it should have been designed a decade earlier. Singapore's more youthful protagonists had a different plan in mind.

Two practitioners in particular – SCDA and WOHA – were the first to articulate an image of the contemporary Singapore tropical house, but the

ABOVE SCDA Architects, Andrew Road House, Singapore, 2003.

architecture was notable for its apparent restraint – not exactly minimal, but most certainly unadorned – and that expression was very much premeditated. Placing restraint upon tropical expression was regarded as questionable to many observers – particularly several outspoken Malaysians, and Tay Kheng Soon himself – but the best designs of that period (not just by SCDA and WOHA) did most adroitly provide Singapore with an image that was really quite suave, not to mention cool, and in that sense the architecture could be seen as a new and undeniably sophisticated expression of tropical urbanity.

With his Sennett Road House of 1990, Soo K. Chan of SCDA flagged the advent of the 'new look' with a tightly orthogonal composition comprised of blade walls, fixed screens of louvres and a carefully calibrated landscape. The house had an assertive and rigidly geometric demeanour, and its passive energy program (ventilation, shading, screening) was almost graphically depicted. Before moving on to bigger things, SCDA (see p. 122) would be prolific at this scale for the next decade, with a formula that was refined and finessed, and which for a time was so instantly recognizable and so widely imitated that it became a cliché.

Wong Mun Summ and Richard Hassell worked together in Kerry Hill's office before setting up WOHA in 1994, and they designed a series of houses over the following eight years that attracted much attention – not only for their appearance and expression, but also for the underlying sustainability of their programmatic intentions (see p. 118). Wong and Hassell were highly accomplished architects, but they were insistent that the parti of their projects was determined by environmental performance, and they later confessed that they 'smuggled in the sustainability without anybody noticing'. They became increasingly uncomfortable with the direction of house design in Singapore, feeling that their prioritization of sustainability would be compromised – the budgets were ever increasing, as were the size of the houses, and, as it almost goes without saying, so were the demands and appetites of the owners. WOHA did not want to run the risk of 'green-washing', and they shifted their attention to public projects. As the money from commissions for mega-houses was being dangled before the eyes of the architects, this was to become an ongoing dilemma, certainly in terms of ethical (sustainable) practice.

It is refreshing, and indeed educational, to look back at those early houses of SCDA and WOHA and note the tight control of their environmentally responsive aesthetic expression, which was enacted in accordance with the client's requirements, even if it was 'smuggled in'. The Singaporean marketplace had provided the opportunity to be cool, calm and decisive, and it served the country well at the time.

ABOVE WOHA, House at Hua Guan Avenue, Singapore, 2001.

GARLICK AVENUE HOUSE

2005
SINGAPORE
KERRY HILL ARCHITECTS

It might seem anomalous in light of the extraordinary influence that he has had over the last thirty years or so, but Kerry Hill designed very few houses, and this discreet yet perfectly realized project is his only remaining house in Singapore. (The Cluny Hill House, completed in 1998, was demolished several years ago.) Hill's significance stems from his hotel and resort designs, which began in the 1970s, and, at a purely architectonic level, there was of course very little difference between the strategies employed for luxurious public accommodation and those for private villas (which were often found in the grounds of the resorts). It is often seen as a mark of disrespect to talk of an architect's 'style', as if it indicates a possibly cynical commodification, but Kerry Hill's style set a benchmark for tropical design, and he never relinquished his mastery of site planning and attention to detail. In retrospect, after a long sequence of vernacular-inflected designs, he settled upon an inimitable style toward the end of the 1990s, when he discarded homage and mimicry in favour of orthogonal abstraction. His architecture remained resolutely tropical, but – much to the delight of critics from colder climes – the forms and planning appeared to be thoroughly modernist. Actually, they were not, as anyone who has spent time in one of his compounds can attest – he had simply devised an uncluttered and deferential method for delighting in a tropical lifestyle, and it paid as many dues to the principles of traditional construction as to those of Mies van der Rohe.

Garlick Avenue House is located at the end of a cul-de-sac in a reasonably affluent, but not exorbitantly wealthy, district of Singapore, and it nestles comfortably into its context of unpretentious free-standing villas shaded by plentiful trees. It might be suggested that the house would not fit so well within the richer enclaves, where even the best-intended architecture must at least hint at a semblance of magnitude, if not ostentation. And therein lies the joy of Hill's architecture – with its scale, use of materials and dexterous planning, the house fits into its site perfectly. It stands on quite a steep slope, from north to south, but that is not apparent within the compound, as the ground plane is completely flat. Now obscured by palm trees, a retaining wall to the north effectively serves as a vertical garden, while a basement and garage lie within the 3-metre (10-foot) drop to the south. The swimming pool, which begins in the entry vestibule as a shallow water feature, cleanly bisects the site from west to east, bounded by a bedroom pavilion and a lawn to the

OPPOSITE AND ABOVE An atrium framed by timber battens rises as a skeletal orthogonal cage above the eastern courtyard and gardens.

north, and the main volume of the house to the south. Below an upper-level gallery, a travertine pool terrace extends from the living and dining room as what may be referred to in traditional terminology as a verandah.

The architecture has two expressions: the first, as viewed from the western entry gardens, has a palatial abstraction with slender vertical elements juxtaposed with a floating roof slab; and the second, as viewed from the internal courtyard, has a delicate yet rigid disposition, defined by the elongated timber battens of a capacious atrium. The graceful proportion and filigree of the atrium, which rises as a skeletal orthogonal 'cage' above the pool terrace, is quietly yet formidably emblematic of Hill's resolution of all that is required for architecture in the tropics. Hill made no more moves than necessary in order to screen, protect and shelter the indoor and outdoor living areas, while simultaneously ordering the relationships between the house and the gardens. An axial orchestration of sightlines continues throughout the architecture and across the site: all views to the gardens from the main volume of the house are framed by the battens and columns of the atrium; the entry pathways have a sequence of right-angled turns that conceal then reveal; and every delineation of the house from its gardens has an orthogonal dimension. Hill has thus engendered what might be described as a Zen-like condition of calm and repose, where the minimal recessive geometry of the architecture provides a backdrop for tropicality to flourish.

TOP An upper-level gallery looks out to the gardens through a screen of timber battens.
ABOVE Looking back from the entry to the western gardens, showing Kerry Hill's axial sequencing of pathways and landscaping.

ABOVE The western elevation has a palatial abstraction, with slender vertical elements juxtaposed with a floating roof slab.

ABOVE View of the eastern entry elevation, showing a curving concrete carapace that serves as roof, wall and floor.

NINETY7 @ SIGLAP

2010
SINGAPORE
AAMER ARCHITECTS

Within Singapore's goal-oriented architecture and design community, Aamer Taher might be regarded as something of a maverick. Laidback, conversationally discursive and apparently untroubled by the exigencies of his profession, he has produced a body of work over the last twenty-five years that is most notable for its eclecticism. Taher has not been one to hit upon a style and stick to it. His houses have variously revealed predilections for modernism, postmodernism, deconstructivism, futurism, featurism, cubism, neoclassicism and expressionism. However, it should be stressed that his dilettante strain is confined purely to the aesthetic. Underneath it all, Taher is fundamentally preoccupied with how to implement the principles of passive energy when designing for the tropics. His architecture is driven by the requirements of catching the breezes, sheltering and screening the interior spaces, reducing the solar load, and, yes, by finding different means of expressing those strategies.

As requested by the client, Ninety7 @ Siglap was ostensibly designed as a party house, and its self-indulgent forms make that intention very clear. Taher refers to it unironically as 'futuristic', thus harking back to those houses of the 1960s and 1970s in which an abundance of curving lines and surfaces reflected the ingenuous optimism of the space age. The forms of futurism were to morph with those of deconstructivism in the 1990s, most conspicuously in the works of Zaha Hadid and Frank Gehry, and a language of wrapping and folding entered the architectural vocabulary. But not so much in the tropics, where the imposition of an enfolding skin seemed singularly inappropriate – blocking off the breezes, trapping the humidity and pretty much demanding the use of air-conditioning. Taher grabbed the look – the flamboyance and dynamism – and he opened it right up, creating a set of 'futuristic' verandahs that extended through the interior spaces from one side to the other.

As the site was located on a small ridge that looks west toward the city, the first thing Taher did was to lift the house off the ground, enabling every level to capture the hilltop breezes. The three levels on the western elevation were arranged both as windcatchers and viewing platforms, supported by a series of angled columns that splay out to exaggerate the cantilevered profile. With more than a hint of Hans Scharoun and Erich Mendelsohn, a sinuous curving geometry – employed both in section and plan – has a nautical 'ocean liner' expression that, enhanced by the wide timber decks, becomes the signature

ABOVE The 'futuristic' forms hark back to the flamboyant stylings of the 1960s and 1970s, as well as those of deconstructivism from the 1990s.

of the architecture. Forming a protective carapace for the entire house, the broad and slender roof swoops down to become a wall before tucking in beneath the floorboards on the second storey. Taher's inclination toward retro-futurism is further revealed in the interior design, with Archizoom-style corridors and bathroom pods, and in the landscape, with a kidney-shaped swimming pool, a circular jacuzzi and an elliptical lawn.

In an award citation, the Singapore Institute of Architects described the design as a 'very up-to-date take on a tropical language of architecture', but it might now be observed that the house was a bit of a one-off. In Singapore especially, the trajectory remains firmly directed by a predisposition to orthogonality, and to a modernism that was not led astray by the Swinging Sixties. Taher, however, prefers to think outside the box when he considers the options: 'Cross-ventilation, natural light, and protection from the climate are now imperative, but we should experiment with fluid and unconventional forms. Although the "boxy" modern house is so popular, we should think about sculpting shapes that are unrelated to those precedents. Architects should be looking for a unique identity, for self-expression, and the freedom to create art.'

ABOVE AND ABOVE RIGHT As befits a party house, the interior design has an avowedly retro and unabashedly hedonistic feel.

OPPOSITE The house is arranged and calibrated to capture the hilltop breezes, which pass through the large gaps in the structure and the open floor plans.

ABOVE AND OPPOSITE A sinuous geometry in both section and plan creates an 'ocean liner' expression.

SARANG HOUSE

2011
SINGAPORE
WOHA

WOHA began as an architectural practice in 1994, when two graduate architects working in Kerry Hill's Singapore office decided to join forces and go out on their own. (The somewhat cryptic name of their firm is in fact an acronym taken from the first two letters of the surnames of Wong Mun Summ and Richard Hassell). They quickly achieved regional prominence through a sequence of houses built in the 1990s, which was glowingly reviewed in what was then a flourishing architectural publication milieu, emanating for the most part from Singapore itself. The houses were strongly, almost uncompromisingly composed, with a very singular eye-catching expression, and they eschewed the use of vernacular tropical language – thus earning, along with the likes of SCDA (see p. 122) and Kerry Hill (see p. 108), the occasionally pejorative epithet of 'tropical modern'. WOHA may have steered resolutely clear of vernacular stylings and features, but it was most assuredly taking its cues from the vernacular principles of passive environmental design, and it was way ahead of the game. Wong and Hassell were truly ambitious, and by the turn of the century they were winning large public projects and had more or less discontinued private house design. WOHA has since flourished at the largest of scales, and its architecture, along with its forays into urban planning, has been consistently underpinned and indeed characterized by its strategies for sustainability.

Several years after this change of typological direction, WOHA did design one more house of note, and it can only really be reviewed in the context of the practice's other work at that time. Wong and Hassell have insisted all along that the application of their fundamental principles has not wavered since the inception of the practice: 'Our approach, our strategies, were scaled up and up. But we haven't changed, we've been very consistent.' And to that end, the monumental, abstracted forms of the Sarang House are quite clearly those of a larger project, used here to disguise and possibly subvert its domestic scale, and when viewed from the street, the house does possess an unusually assertive and self-assured demeanour. As with their early houses, the architects were not inclined to compromise with a concession to suburban context or, far more importantly, a diminishment of environmental performance. The appearance of the Sarang House was not simply delineated as an expression of their strategies for passive energy design – it was instead used to create what can be appreciated as a new aesthetic, that of sustainability.

OPPOSITE When viewed from the street, the house has a monumental abstracted form. Sheer planar walls reduce solar gain on the exposed northern elevation. **ABOVE** The timber façades of the end elevations are juxtaposed with the metal rods of the lengthy southern elevation.

The long and narrow hilltop site presented an immediate challenge, as it was completely exposed on the north to the heat of the sun, while shrouded by trees to the south. The architecture makes an aesthetic virtue of this environmental distinction by devising a house with two faces, with two expressions. The northern section, containing circulation routes and services, is shielded from the sun by a set of planar whitewashed walls, relieved by a trim of grey stone and precast concrete. By contrast, the living areas to the south open out directly to the gardens, with an upper level screened by a delicately filigreed framework of timber and metal strips (the word *sarang* means 'nest' in Malay, and the bedrooms are indeed nestled within this latticework). Perhaps the most captivating aspect of the design is the attention paid to the details: the arrangement of the metal rods in the external framework, the rustication of the grey stonework, the staggered stacking of the white walls and the quality of the timber joinery found throughout the interiors. At the time, WOHA was working on several upmarket resorts (most notably Alila Villas Uluwatu and the Sanya InterContinental) as interior designers as well as architects, and that degree of finesse and crafted artfulness was patently permeating all the practice's work.

ABOVE Screened by a filigreed framework of timber and metal strips on the southern elevation, the living areas open out to trees and gardens.

TOP AND ABOVE Screens and structural perforations throughout provide cross-ventilation.

TOP AND ABOVE A staggered, sliding geometry is used for the walls of the northern elevation and the gardens below.

HEEREN SHOPHOUSE

1999
MELAKA, MALAYSIA
SCDA ARCHITECTS

Melaka was one of the great trade-route entrepôts, sitting midway on the Straits that bear its name, and its historic heart remains charmingly intact – not just in terms of architectural conservation, but also in its cultural ambience. Spreading out from the banks of its muddy, somewhat sluggish and rather indolent river, the civic edifices built by the colonial rulers, and the mercantile and residential buildings erected by all manner of settlers with a vested interest, maintain a beguiling and delightfully antiquated comportment. The two main streets of the Chinese district, running west from the river and known until recently as Jonker and Heeren streets, form one of the most authentic time capsules to be found anywhere in tropical Asia. The Baba Nyonya[1] way of living continues without affectation – perfumed smoke from joss sticks fills the air, bowls of laksa are served in tiled and noisy street-front restaurants, and the shop owners often prefer to use an abacus. With some dating back to the seventeenth century, the façades of the arcaded two-storey shophouses on the narrow length of Heeren Street have been preserved without significant disfigurement, and one of them serves as the portal to a most ingenious internal renovation – one which can only really be described as an installation.

The internal structure of a century-old Chinese shophouse had collapsed, and the cavernous high-walled space had lingered derelict, unused and roofless for many years. The renovation was not intended to restore the structure as a domestic and/or commercial space, so much as to create a 'stage-set', a place imbued with mystery and nostalgia that might inspire metaphysical contemplation. As a sanctuary for meditation, a small pavilion was erected where there was once an open courtyard in the centre of the shophouse's elongated plan, and it 'floats', cantilevered above

OPPOSITE An elevated pavilion is placed toward the rear of the narrow high-walled enclosure.
ABOVE Looking back to the street front. The burnt-out and rundown remnants of the original structure are retained as signifiers of a specific cultural history.

ABOVE Timber-framed living quarters above the space previously occupied by the street-front shop.

a rectangular pool. Reflected in symmetry within the narrow confines of the dilapidated shell, the very contemporary lines and proportions of the pavilion serve as the focal point for a space where the burnt-out and rundown remnants of the shophouse were retained as artefacts, as signifiers of cultural history and the passage of time. Chinese characters and ornamental tiles form part of the charred patina of the old street-front shop, and the blank peeling walls appear as if scumbled – pockmarked by sheered-off brickwork and slots for rotted timber beams. Steel I-beams brace the walls and support the pavilion, as well as a living space built from slatted timber, which was erected above the shopfront and reached by a spiral staircase of black-painted steel.

It is the delineation of the soaring though diminutive pavilion that reveals the hand of the architect, Soo K. Chan, who grew up in Penang – the other great trading port on the west coast of the Malay Peninsula. After studying and working for many years in the USA, Chan set up SCDA in Singapore in 1995, and he quickly became one of the region's leading lights. He was widely acclaimed (and much imitated) for an architecture described by Philip Goad as 'a distinctive interpretation of modernism, emphasising horizontality through dramatic oversailing eaves and hovering prismatic forms.'[2] Within the ruins of the shophouse on Heeren Street, the installation of that crisp clean orthogonality worked only too perfectly – the space was not just utilized as a place for contemplation and existential timelessness, but as an architectural showcase. On the one hand, the architect had preserved the decay and dilapidation, while on the other, in its midst, he had imposed a purified rendition of modernism. The pavilion is displayed as a pristine object, as if it had been deposited – landed from above – on a movie set depicting a primeval civilization, and the architectural connotations of that juxtaposition were quite profound. As Ng Seksan remarked at the time, 'What a paradigm shift that was,' and he, among others, would take great inspiration from the possibilities suggested by its phenomenological juxtapositions.

ABOVE The crisply detailed modernist pavilion floats as a place for contemplation within the shell of the dilapidated shophouse.

NASSIM HOUSE

2020
SINGAPORE
STUDIOMILOU

In personality and in social outlook, Jean-François Milou is an embodiment, almost to the point of caricature, of the generation of French architects that flourished in the era of the *grands projets*, those who saw the requirement for civic grandeur as a noble obligation. Milou was born in 1953, his father a philosopher, his mother a poet. He studied at the Ecole nationale supérieure des Beaux-Arts in Paris, and, until he was commissioned for Nassim House, he had only designed public buildings in France (most notably the transformation of the historic covered market Carreau du Temple in Paris), Vietnam and Singapore, where he won the competition for the National Gallery in 2007. He also works as a consultant for UNESCO, advising on conservation and adaptive re-use in countries such as Georgia, Nepal and India, and as he makes clear in conversation, his feeling for architecture is of a cultural tradition, informed by archaeology, philosophy, history and all the visual arts. He is, in short, a Renaissance man now plying his trade in an age of digital algorithms and artificial intelligence.

Shortly after the completion of National Gallery Singapore in 2015 to widespread acclaim, Milou was commissioned by a prominent banking and philanthropic family to design a large house in the Nassim Road area of Singapore, a stately, heavily treed enclave with gracious villas often occupied by foreign embassies. Milou's explanations of the design process take the form of self-quizzical soliloquies and philosophical ruminations, and he recounts his intentions and subsequent assessment as if such retrospective analysis forms part of the construction cycle:

> Singapore must convey its beauty, that's why I made a sculpture for the trees, where we are 'sous bois'...under the trees and in the shadows. The colonnades have an awkward verticality, they are not abstract, because I wanted to create tension. I imagined that the house was being cast in bronze, and I wanted it monolithic and enigmatic, and delicate and unified. I always want to make things more complex...

LEFT AND ABOVE A ceremonial lawn is placed between the private residence at the rear of the site (left) and the public living pavilion (above).

> avoid the functional, the rational, and the industrial. And I like to come up with things that are horribly difficult to assemble, but really simple to look at. There is craft, but much more than that, there is art. For me, the satisfaction is in the process, and it's a social process...I like those stories of the Balinese temples, where they document the design and construction through to completion, and then there is no more use for the building. But when I look at my work like that, I sometimes think I don't understand what I'm doing.

Nassim House was built on a plot of land that had been hived off from the grounds of the splendid Eden Hall, home to the British High Commissioner. It was implicit that studioMilou had been chosen because the family regularly entertained a large number of guests – the house and its gardens would effectively need to serve as a public venue, much in the manner of an embassy. As its northwestern boundary had been determined by the sweep of Eden Hall's driveway, the site had an anomalous proportion – shaped rather like an elongated grand piano, it tapered from a curvaceous swell into a narrow rectangle at the rear, where there was a surprisingly steep hillside. That hillside was excavated to form a quarry, which would house a capacious and very private residence, separated by a ceremonial lawn from an entertainment and living pavilion bounded by Nassim Road to the south.

Milou took inspiration from the majestic verticality of the trees that abound in the Nassim area, and he conceived a sculptural architectural expression that took the form of a sequence of colonnades screening the two pavilions and a winding pathway on the site's northwestern edge. The colonnades were composed of slender vertical concrete 'planks', which had been pressed in relief by sawn pine timber and arrayed in a wilfully haphazard manner, as if groves of spindly trees. The glass-clad volumes of the two pavilions are effectively hidden by the colonnades, and as studioMilou was not commissioned for the interior design, the aesthetic expression was purely external, and should perhaps be regarded as landscape architecture. The lawn was fringed by dark-green hoop pines with a broad and unruly spread of branches, and their juxtaposition with the colonnades presents a memorable, if unlikely, tableau. (Milou states that the pines were the client's idea – he wanted broad-leaf trees that would merge with those of the neighbourhood, but he concedes that the elemental contrast has been very effective.) The overall impression of the landscape is possibly more Roman than anything else – one thinks of the cypresses and ancient colonnades of the Forum and the Palatino – and the artfully contrived ambience of 'organicized' classicism represents an intriguing response to a requirement for civic grandeur in the tropics.

ABOVE Slender concrete columns have been pressed in relief by sawn pine timber.

ABOVE Small pathways wind around the circumference of the site, framed by concrete colonnades and hoop pines.

ABOVE A reflection pool adjoining the living pavilion is enclosed by the organicized colonnades and the trees of the Nassim area.

OVERLEAF A lengthy colonnade on the northwestern boundary wraps around the central lawn and gardens.

TROPICAL EXPRESSION

'Architects who work with abstract compositions might think they are tapping into the zeitgeist, but I just think they are missing out on all the fun.' REX ADDISON[1]

It was Jimmy Lim who said that he simply wanted to design houses as private resorts, and it was Ernesto Bedmar (see p. 186) who went on to compose and arrange the most sumptuous gardens of tropical delight for those who had the wealth and taste. Bedmar trained as an architect in Córdoba, Argentina, and initially worked in Soweto, South Africa, on a housing project designed by his compatriot and mentor, Miguel Ángel Roca. He then moved to Hong Kong, where he linked up with the renowned Portuguese architect, Álvaro Siza, to work on the conservation of Macau's historic quarter, before heading down to Singapore in 1986, where he quickly fell into a deep and abiding love affair with the tropics. His subsequent architecture has been nothing less than an exuberant, not to say sensual, manifestation of that lingering infatuation:

> I developed a heartfelt reverence for the values of Southeast Asia, and, at the same time, I stumbled upon a profound architectural precept – only the roof and columns are essential...we can live without the rest. My love for this landscape – its textures, smell, and humidity – deepened. The idea of embracing it, containing it, yet liberating it, were constant preoccupations for me.[2]

Bedmar's earlier houses were adroit and innovative variations upon the Bali style, and the artfulness of Geoffrey Bawa was clearly apparent, but he was taking note of concurrent developments in Singapore's architecture. The design of Victoria Park House in 2000 was demonstrably influenced by the work of SCDA (see p. 122) and Kerry Hill (see p. 108), featuring textured walls of stone with slot windows, fixed screens of battened timber, and clean-edged rectilinear landscaping. He quickly moved on, establishing his own imprint, and his next set of houses demonstrated a compositional and material mastery that has in many ways become the very image of the tropical house. The details of his approach do not really need to be explained in architectural jargon, one only needs to look at the photographs, or as Wong Mun Summ from WOHA (see p. 118) commented: 'I don't think about the architecture, I just want to live in one of his houses'.

ABOVE Ernesto Bedmar Architects, Sadeesh House, Subang Jaya, Malaysia, 2002.

Unless the architect or builder 'cheats' – by sealing off everything and turning up the air-conditioning – the methods for providing shelter, shade and ventilation in the tropics have an inherently expressive quality. Tall pitched roofs, broad overhangs, projecting eaves, elevated verandahs, slender columns and overscaled windows and doors all contrive (often unwittingly) to provide an aesthetic that in the hands of certain architects, and vernacular craftsmen, should actually be described as 'expressionist'. Tropical architecture might thus be seen as a virtuous artform, deriving a dynamic and seemingly exaggerated composition from the articulation of its program for environmental sustainability. In other words, contemporary architects can reiterate what the Minangkabau of Sumatra and the Toraja of Sulawesi have been doing for centuries. Bedmar did not specifically borrow elements or styles from the vernacular, but he adopted its 'expressionist' parti to devise houses-as-resorts, where all the aesthetic and tactile pleasures of the environment and his architecture were enhanced in an innately compatible manner.

As most contemporary modes of expression have not set out to mimic the forms of a specifically localized vernacular (it was more a case of being unable not to do so, they were inherent and intrinsic), the processes of cross-fertilization in regional design and construction continue, as they always have. The architects from the Brisbane region who so vigorously resisted the suffocating influence of provincial modernism back in the 1970s, were initially motivated by re-establishing the spirit of their regional non-indigenous vernacular of 'timber and tin' – the humble, unpretentious, but charming structures that had been built to withstand the environmental hardships and economic privations of the nineteenth century. The source of the vernacular was then extended when Russell Hall (see p. 46) and Rex Addison (see p. 50) worked in Papua New Guinea, and brought back a new appreciation of structural possibilities. (It might be noted in passing that Hall, whose work was nearly always built from timber and tin, asserts that his greatest influence was Antoni Gaudí, while Addison claims the same of Frank Lloyd Wright.)

Interest in tropical design has dwindled in Australia over the last two decades (a curious state of affairs), but Charles Wright, based in Port Douglas – which is about as far north and tropical as you can get 'down under' – has produced a series of remarkable houses, which, not least by his own reckoning, take their cue from the likes of John Lautner. As opposed to the work of his predecessors in Brisbane, Wright sought a monumental expression, often in exposed concrete, with vast indoor/outdoor spaces, great brooding all-encompassing roofs, and an inclination to treat his projects as a form of land art (see p. 138). It is indeed difficult to ascertain any tangible connection to earlier architecture in northern Australia, and as his houses were consummately tropicalized in every aspect of their conception, Wright does not fit into any purview of current Australian architecture – his peer group lies across the water to the northwest.

As can be frequently observed behind the walls and hedges of the leafiest enclaves in Singapore, Guz Wilkinson 'specializes' in houses with a very distinctive tropical expression (see p. 164). When he set up practice in 1996, he initially indulged himself by designing bungalows in the manner of Charles Voysey and Edwin Lutyens, but as he recalls, 'I soon realized that I was stuck doing Arts and Crafts when Singapore wanted contemporary modern'. Wilkinson's trick was to fuse the two, and, in doing that, he created something altogether new. Fish House, designed in 2006 (completed in 2009), was a startling breakthrough: a bijou waterfront house, elegantly crafted in a nautical manner with huge overhanging eaves and continuous revealed circulation routes, and each of his subsequent houses has elaborated on that parti. He has, however, never strayed from the fundamental sentiments of the Arts and Crafts movement, often declaring that 'the garden is more important than the house'.

ABOVE Charles Wright, The Edge House, Port Douglas, Australia, 2014.

The 'expressionist' iteration of the idyllic tropical house does not comprise as many remarkable pieces of architecture as one might imagine. Only too often, the designs of houses-as-private-resorts veered into kitsch, confusion and downright bad taste (much as they did with the actual resorts themselves), and even in the hands of the best architects, the inevitable tendency to over-build, and to defy the circumscriptions of an urban site, sucked all the romanticism out of the air. When the idyll was realized, however, the creations could be appreciated as glorious one-offs (much in the manner of the grand palazzos of yore, to which they effectively constitute an update), and here a common thread must be noted – the architect and client had a relationship in sympatico. A grand piece of architecture, which cannot help but verge upon self-indulgence on both sides, could hardly be achieved in the face of disagreement or disinterest.

Sinurambi (see p. 182), high up in the ranges radiating from Mount Kinabalu, was designed in 2001 by young Malaysian architect Ling Fahshing as a tribute to, and reinterpretation of, the vernacular structures of Borneo. Looming large above the rainforest as though a hunting lodge or tribal headquarters, it was conceived in a most heartening collaboration with Fahshing's clients. A similarly resolute intention to reaffirm the expressionism of vernacular forms lay behind Lok Kuang Wooi's design for his family home, built in 2003 in Shah Alam (see p. 30). Slender brick walls, vertical timber elements, finely battened screens and slot windows are arrayed and layered beneath a soaring roof as elements in a rustic form of repetitive mannerism. In the same year, John Heah produced a magnificently crafted one-of-a-kind in the salubrious Coronation Road West area of Singapore, and it was the ultimate house-as-resort, if not palace, with extravagant mouldings and elaborate timber cabinet work (see p. 170). The Bond House, designed by Alexis Dornier in 2018 for one of those breathtakingly beautiful sites above a gorge in Bali, has a similar disposition of aesthetic purity and compositional harmony, and it was conceived as the ultimate party house (see p. 148). Cantilevered bridges and platforms reach out to the bucolic-cum-celestial panorama, and their fascias, clad in pale green Javanese stone, comprise the only assertion of 'architecture'. The house and the vista prompt one to quietly ask: Dare architects intrude when they are working in paradise?

TOP John Heah, Malcomson-Clayton House, Singapore, 2003. **ABOVE** Alexis Dornier, Bond House, Bali, Indonesia, 2020.

ABOVE Guz Architects, Fish House, Singapore, 2009.

STAMP HOUSE

2013
CAPE TRIBULATION, AUSTRALIA
CHARLES WRIGHT

A refugee from the chilly winter winds of Melbourne, Charles Wright has been practising in Far North Queensland for over twenty years, and he remains most cheerfully and gratefully immersed in that region's geographical and societal dispositions. This is a land where the mountains meet the sea, the rainforests and cane fields are verdant and beautiful, the breezes are languid and blissful, and the residents have a relaxed and carefree countenance. Commissioned to provide houses that celebrate the lifestyle of pleasure without restraint, Wright grasped the opportunity to devote himself in a most single-minded and highly expressive manner to the principles and the practice of tropical architecture. The startling formal flamboyance of Wright's work is as much

a response to the environment and the climate as it is to his aesthetic inclinations. His architecture delights in the elaborations of structural necessity and revels in the luxuriance of the landscape, yet the designs are researched and conceived as prototypes for tropical living, wherein the voids of the section and the incisions of the plan are calibrated for comprehensive natural ventilation and protection from the elements.

Wright has paid scant regard to the mores of Australian establishment architecture, yet he has also abstained from the prevailing 'lightweight' approach of a previous generation who had worked in the tropics. On no account did he deviate from the fundamental climatic and sustainable principles applied by such architects as Troppo (see p. 24), Russell Hall (see p. 46), Rex Addison (see p. 50) and Gabriel Poole, but he employs massing to withstand and shield in the harsh environment – he uses concrete, not 'timber and tin'. His built works possess an energy, a monumentality and a robust tectonic confidence that place him firmly in the lineage of Oscar Niemeyer, Eero Saarinen and John Lautner. With a resolutely tropical sense of place and a defiantly self-assured compositional poise, his architecture should really be positioned alongside the works of contemporary Southeast Asian and Central American practitioners, rather than those of his own country.

At Cape Tribulation – which is as far north as it is possible to drive on the east coast of Australia without risking a broken axle – Stamp House is set on a narrow coastal strip beneath the brooding peaks of the Daintree mountain range, and if ever an architectural commission could be described as a one-off, this is it. In an isolated and wondrously beautiful location, Wright had been presented with an open-ended brief from his client, whereupon he could respond with alacrity to produce something much more than a mere house, and the completed structure should really be appreciated as a public building (one is tempted to suggest that it might eventually serve as a visitor's centre, museum or gallery). Rather than acquiesce and defer to the ever-looming grandeur of the mountains and the velvet splendour of the rainforests on their slopes, Stamp House reciprocates and reiterates as a topographical intervention. It could perhaps be appreciated as a work of land art whose overscaled silhouette is rendered supremely graphic by its reflection in the waters below.

The 26-hectare (64-acre) site, previously a cattle farm, was cleared to form a lake, or more accurately a moat, which now wraps around an island house – a concrete mass with five quasi-tubular protrusions that spear out and fan over the waters in a star-shaped configuration. Those cantilevered pods, containing bedrooms and a kitchen, enclose a vast living room that is

PREVIOUS PAGE AND ABOVE Located on a disused cattle farm in the spectacular Daintree region of Far North Queensland, the house is placed on an island in a newly formed lake.

ABOVE Five living pods thrust out over the waters in a star-shaped configuration.

roofed but not walled, and centred by a swimming pool open to the sky. The living area is a community space in the great tradition of tropical vernacular architecture – the airflow is balmy and constant, reflected daylight bounces in from the lake and the pool, and any non-tempestuous rainfall serves as a pleasantly diverting cooling device. The high ceilings form a bravura showpiece of structural expressionism whose geometries and coffered dimensions appear as wilfully eccentric and mannerist – triangulated and distended with a wayward grid. Externally, the thrusting profiles of the five pods look set for lift-off, with the perforations in the concrete arrayed as if rivets in a Lockheed fuselage. Wright worked closely with his client, a stamp dealer named Rod Perry (who sadly died shortly after the house was completed), and the seemingly whimsical shape of the swimming pool was derived from the proud 'aboriginal warrior' profile of Gwoya Jungarai, featured on the classic 'One Pound Jimmy' postage stamp released in 1950.

TOP AND OPPOSITE Much in the vein of John Lautner, the coffered concrete ceilings form a showpiece of structural expressionism.

ABOVE A swimming pool and courtyard in the centre of the house are left open to the elements.

P3 HOUSE

2003
PRAN BURI, THAILAND
KANIKA R'KUL ARCHITECT

In comparison to its Southeast Asian peer group – specifically Malaysia, Singapore and Indonesia – it could be observed that Thailand had the least assertive and most tentative architecture culture at the turn of the twenty-first century. With such a rich and seductive array of histories – not least in the fields of art, design and public building – one might have expected a few flashes of flair and flamboyance, but somewhat puzzlingly, there was little that pointed to any self-reflexive considerations of local identity. Nor were there any notable manifestations of what one might hope to see as typically Thai in a contemporary sense: colourful, extroverted and aesthetically polyglot. The exuberance and the multi-layered rhythms and complexities of Bangkok's street life, for example, were not reflected in the city's architecture. Elsewhere in the region, architects (often in intellectual collaboration, such as Arsitek Muda Indonesia, Young Architects of Indonesia, see p. 247) had focused on geopolitical realities and the direction of a new urbanity, both in terms of expression and social responsibility. The best of those architects attempted to interpret the momentous recent changes in their countries' circumstances, to respond and adapt with programmatic and architectonic panache, but their Thai counterparts appeared to lie confused.

When Kanika R'Kul spoke at the Arcasia Forum in 2001, she bemoaned the status of Thai architecture in no uncertain terms: 'The general feeling is that the effect of the globalized economy and Western-dominated mass media has progressively contaminated and eradicated the "Thai-ness" in every aspect of our culture. And architecture is no exception. I don't view our identity as having been lost, but it has been rather drastically transformed – so drastic that it has become difficult to recognize.' Born in Bangkok, R'Kul trained as an architect in the USA and worked there and in Germany before returning to Thailand in 1995, when, as she confesses, she felt somewhat distanced from and frustrated by what appeared to be well-entrenched modes of practice and critical thinking. R'Kul was not a revolutionary, not even a polemicist in the manner of Malaysia's Kevin Low, but her small projects were quietly yet forcefully considered and self-assured – the program and performance of the houses were clearly delineated, and they attracted much attention. Her clarity of intent was refreshing – a circuit breaker of sorts – and when seen in the contested context of a localized scramble for identity, it did denote a tangible progression.

OPPOSITE Seen from the western entry, the house is split in two by a timber deck and a viewing platform. **TOP** View from the beach showing the transparent cubic volumes of the two pavilions. **ABOVE** Looking out to the Gulf of Thailand from the central viewing platform.

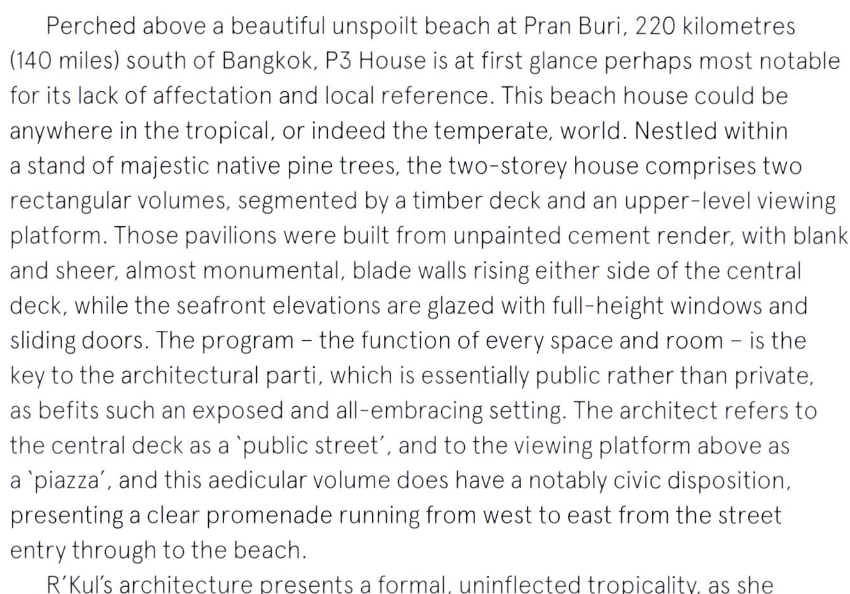

Perched above a beautiful unspoilt beach at Pran Buri, 220 kilometres (140 miles) south of Bangkok, P3 House is at first glance perhaps most notable for its lack of affectation and local reference. This beach house could be anywhere in the tropical, or indeed the temperate, world. Nestled within a stand of majestic native pine trees, the two-storey house comprises two rectangular volumes, segmented by a timber deck and an upper-level viewing platform. Those pavilions were built from unpainted cement render, with blank and sheer, almost monumental, blade walls rising either side of the central deck, while the seafront elevations are glazed with full-height windows and sliding doors. The program – the function of every space and room – is the key to the architectural parti, which is essentially public rather than private, as befits such an exposed and all-embracing setting. The architect refers to the central deck as a 'public street', and to the viewing platform above as a 'piazza', and this aedicular volume does have a notably civic disposition, presenting a clear promenade running from west to east from the street entry through to the beach.

R'Kul's architecture presents a formal, uninflected tropicality, as she prefers quite pragmatically to devote her energies to maximizing the potential of the site and the intended program without imposing any suggestion of iconography or symbolism, and there is not even a hint of ornament and decoration. It is, if you like, an architecture of the tabula rasa, a chance to begin again. As R'Kul said in 2001, reiterating her personal aversion to bad decision-making and bad habits in Thai culture, her underlying intention is: 'How to be useful, so that a new sense of "Thai-ness" might emerge. So, one step at a time, I suppose.'

LEFT Kanika R'Kul did not intend the beach house to be designed as a private hideaway, referring to the upper deck as a 'public piazza'. **ABOVE** The living areas open out to the beach through full-height windows and sliding doors.

BOND HOUSE

2020
UBUD, BALI, INDONESIA
ALEXIS DORNIER

It was not named after James Bond, but it could have been. A hideaway in paradise designed for the jet set, and quite conceivably for a cast of playboys, villains and spies. But the reference was purely literal – the bond was between people and nature. The owner, Kyan, has a background in music, clubbing and entrepreneurial enterprise in his native Germany, and he is happy to be described as a businessman who likes to party, and, it would appear, as a man who has made partying his business. At that occasionally transcendental but essentially sybaritic level where lifestyle comprises revelry and/or the unfettered indulgence in material delights, Bali has been and always will be Shangri La, and many architects over the years have not been shy in their response. As Philip Goad wrote of the best of the Balinese resorts: 'They are skilful and highly resolved exercises in appealing to the most profound wants in Western society's eyes – the pleasures of the threshold; the pleasures of the perception of an exotic "other"; and the pleasures of being in a highly sensitised state, and in what better place than Bali, Island of the Gods?'[1]

There are many precedents for Bond House, in spirit if not architectural style. One need look no further than artist Donald Friend's 1970s Batujimbar estate, where Geoffrey Bawa assisted in the design of several villas erected for no other reason than the promulgation of the party (visitors apparently included Princess Soraya of Iran, Gore Vidal, Mick Jagger and the Duke of Edinburgh).[2] In such settings, as noted by Goad, the pleasure of the threshold is intrinsic to the architecture of welcome, and the entry sequence to Bond House is one of unfolding delight: the journey to Ubud from the airport forms

LEFT View of the entry, showing the symmetrical layering of the roof terraces above the living areas. **ABOVE** It was intended that the roof be used as a dance floor and a stage set for concerts.

a gradual ascent through the rice terraces; the ever-narrowing road to the house terminates in a high-walled enclosure at the top edge of a gorge, whereupon the gates swing open, and a panoramic view of the valley and the jungle is framed in perfect symmetry by the house itself. Bond House is thus, on first impression, something of a non-house, a deferential composition of discreet architectural elements that were, as Kyan explains, designed to 'blur and merge with nature so it all becomes one entity'. Upon further exploration, however, the architecture reveals itself to be quite formidable, resolute and tectonically resolved, making a virtue of an industrial-style monochromatic minimalism – a deliberate typological transposition of the factories and warehouses of Kreuzberg in Berlin, where Kyan's generation had worked and partied hard.

Alexis Dornier, the architect, is also from Germany, and in his hands the typological and tectonic references are quite specific – to Peter Behrens, to the early buildings of Walter Gropius and most significantly to the masterworks of Ludwig Mies van der Rohe. The only overt manifestation of architectural expression is to be seen in the gantry-style footbridges, which are clad by panels of pale green andesite[3] whose mottled tonal patterning suggests nothing less than those of Mies's Barcelona Pavilion, while the floating slab that roofs the entire house was directly inspired by the Neue Nationalgalerie in Berlin, the last great building by Mies. As Dornier grappled with the challenges of the site's precipitous slope and with Kyan's explicit brief, the concept design process underwent seven separate iterations over four months, but the essential parti was clear from the outset: the massive roof slab was the fundament from which all else followed, or descended, as it were. The big move was to break away from the presumed horizontal plan and extend the floorplate as a T-shape, with a 26-metre (85-foot) swimming pool that cantilevered over the valley to provide an extremely photogenic 'instagrammable' vision of tropical luxury and splendour. Straddled by three gantries/walkways, the pool surmounts a spa in a darkened grotto with monolithic walls – a nightclub-style netherworld that looks out to the jungle on either side through huge circular windows.

ABOVE The panels of pale green andesite, a stone sourced from Java, merge compatibly with the lush landscape.

ABOVE The swimming pool extends from the rectangular plan as a T-shape, cantilevered high over the gorge.

ABOVE Looking up from the valley below. The bedrooms are placed on the lower level, beneath the dining and entertainment areas.

Possibly the most pertinent remark made b architecture and the residential lifestyle, is th house is occupied by successive waves of th twenty-four-hour party people – some qui – for whom the spaces serve as venues to the day. As the house looks to the east, t contemplation; midday is for the poolsi sunset is up on the roof; and night-time is

The ground floor comprises two open-plan livin manipulated to suit, whether for quiet dinners or raucous pa roof was always visualized to be a dancefloor, and a stage-set for conc performances and fashion parades. Bond House was thus intended as palatial accommodation for a community, rather than a family, but, as the architect and owner point out, it functions perfectly well as a house anyway. At a certain level –where hedonism is lifestyle – the definition of a house strays from conventional notions of domesticity, and, in the sense of communal bonding, Bond House marks a reversion to the traditional (and very Balinese) typology of gathering spaces built for kinship, rather than family.

ABOVE The private, secluded bedrooms are adjoined by a basement spa in a darkened grotto.

ABOVE The open-plan living areas can be configured to suit, whether for quiet dinners or raucous jungle parties.

FILMMAKER'S HOUSE

2001
ALIBAG, INDIA
RAHUL MEHROTRA ARCHITECTS

Rahul Mehrotra set up practice in Mumbai in 1990, just as India's socio-economic pendulum swung from a residually feudalized form of socialism to a tentative embrace of free-market capitalism. As seen in many other recently independent and slowly emerging countries, an initial program of nation-building conflated with an improvement in social equity was being redirected by the forces of globalization and middle-class aspiration. Mehrotra recalls that architectural practice of the time was operating in 'the landscape of impatient capital', and it must be observed that most attempts to establish a sense of 'Indian' architectural identity have been subsequently thwarted by the intrinsic confusions of that landscape. Mehrotra is venerated as an academic and author, one who has documented and analyzed India's urbanity and society while simultaneously practising as an architect. He describes contemporary India as 'a muddle of many things' – a succinct observation that takes pretty much everything (history, society, economy, culture) into account, including architecture.

Trained in Ahmedabad before obtaining a Master's degree from the Graduate School of Design at Harvard in 1987, Mehrotra had from the outset a very worldly view of architecture, and he was fundamentally motivated by its social role in an ever-fluctuating urban environment, specifically that of Mumbai, where he served as executive director of the Urban Design Research Institute, and founded a conservation practice. His own architecture displayed a not-unexpected erudition, carefully blending a variety of styles and sources to provide an expression that was simultaneously global and local, and thus a reflection of its time, which has possibly not yet passed. His architecture though, is not 'a muddle of many things' – it is considered and restrained, directed by an awareness of the interaction between spaces and material usage, and a deference to the immediate environment.

Designed and built as a retreat, two hours' drive from Mumbai in the semi-rural environs of Alibag, Filmmaker's House can now be appreciated (over twenty years later) as an exemplar of an approach that was pervading the upper echelons of architectural thinking in the region at the time. Mehrotra's design bears immediate comparison with the contemporaneous work of Kevin Low in Kuala Lumpur, Andra Matin in Jakarta and Cheong Yew Kuan in Bali. All four architects were preoccupied with a search for an architecture that unambiguously understood and acknowledged its culture and context, but

LEFT Responding to the dry and dusty landscape, the architecture is robust and elemental, making a virtue of the tectonic interplay between stone, steel and masonry.

which was indisputably of its time. It was an approach that was rather loosely referred to as 'critical regionalism' – including as it did architecture from the Arctic Circle alongside that of the Greek Islands and Arizona – but in the newly emergent 'landscapes of impatient capital' in tropical Asia, it did have a profound resonance. Well-versed in global architectural developments, each of those architects was intellectually aware and formally gifted, and the best of their work has a quiet authority and a measured, unconflicted sense of place.

Sited in a dry and dusty landscape, Filmmaker's House has a presence that accentuates the benignly pleasurable attributes of that environment. The architecture is robust and elemental, making a virtue – both inside and out – of the tectonic interplay between stone, steel and masonry, and it is clear that Mehrotra was aware of contemporaneous work in Mexico and Portugal, for example. Jutting out from the thick stone wall that comprises the entire eastern elevation, the skillion roof above the entry verandah has a quasi-heroic avionic profile, establishing a contrast of juxtaposition that is somehow enigmatic yet symbolic. That rather indefinable ambience of shaded ambiguity is continued through the large circulation-cum-living areas of the house, where the discolourations of rough construction are counteracted by highly polished floors and elegantly surfaced walls. As befits a house for a filmmaker, all these spaces are spot-lit, by circular skylights and deep windows with coloured reveals.

As with his regional peer group, Mehrotra had something of a blank slate to work on, as India had not yet established a trajectory of modern house design. As to whether his architecture is identifiably Indian is probably best answered in regard to its specific context, that of a certain arid tropicality, where the heat and the rain are kept at bay with mass and containment. The fortified exterior forms enclose an intriguing, yet cool and refreshing, netherworld – an architectural parti that does have many centuries of precedence in subcontinental proximity.

ABOVE The east-facing verandah is surmounted by a skillion roof with a swooping avionic profile.

TOP Alluding to the Indian histories of monumental construction, the external forms have a fortified appearance.

TOP RIGHT, ABOVE LEFT AND ABOVE RIGHT The circulation spaces and living areas have a mysterious, theatrical ambience.

PIANG DAO RETREAT

2014
CHIANG DAO, THAILAND
CSYA

Piang Dao Retreat was the brainchild of Colin Okashimo, a landscape architect turned public artist whose inspirations have emerged from self-assigned exercises in introspection and philosophical deliberation. Unsurprisingly, meditation has long been part of that process, and with a collection of fellow devotees he purchased a plot of hillside land in northern Thailand with a view to creating 'a place for the mind to be challenged or rested through contemplation, meditation and reflection'. It was a view of a different kind that determined the selection of the site itself, which looked across bucolic forested fields to Doi Luang Chiang Dao, a great brooding mountain revered as one of the most sacred in Thailand. And what a view it is. As one gazes, almost hypnotically, to the west from the retreat, the moods of the mountain are a sight to behold – facial expressions come and go in the most fleeting fashion, wrapped and rewrapped by swirling shrouds of cloud, swooping bands of rain and flickering patches of sunlight.

Okashimo asked an old friend, the much-esteemed Malaysian architect Sonny Chan, to work with him at Piang Dao. As Okashimo recalls, their initial and decisive site meeting took the form of an exploratory adventure: 'We climbed up and down the mountain and discovered temples that were embedded in the slopes. Many were in caves, and we felt that our architectural forms should also feel like they were part of the earth.' After many years of working on large-scale projects as a partner with Kumpulan Akitek, Chan set up CSYA as his own practice in Singapore in 1993, and his architecture clearly evinced a fine eye and a cool head. He eschewed wanton expressiveness in favour of an elemental correctness of form and proportion, and he settled upon off-form concrete as his medium, but it was never used brutally or aggressively. The buildings reposed in harmony within their tropical settings, with walls, roofs and columns that were reticent, reserved and classically disposed.

The architecture of the Piang Dao compound is inordinately reticent and reserved, comprising just two pavilions on a linear plan that offers a

LEFT AND ABOVE The two pavilions are architecturally reticent, deferring to the immediate landscape and the sweeping panoramas of northern Thailand.

continuous view of the mountain to the west, a vista that is always framed and partially concealed by rows and groves of trees. Despite their reluctance to show off, to say 'look at me', the buildings are quietly monumental, deriving power and charm – in the Doric manner – from the sobriety and robustness of their forms. Okashimo describes the architecture as, 'very much in scale with the landscape. It was sympathetic to the topography, and it emphasized the experience of being in the spaces. Sonny focused on simplicity of form, and his structures blended into a very quiet context...they nearly disappeared, but not quite.'

Both pavilions are pretty much invisible on approach: the roofs are carpeted with trumpet vines, so the landscape quite literally encroaches upon the architecture. The pitched and very wide-spreading roofs envelope the darkened bedrooms and living areas (all the ceilings are stained black), and as per the original design intentions, all the interior spaces feel like they are indeed part of the earth, as caverns that retreat and recede into the hillside.

The architecture and the landscape are fundamentally intertwined, one might say conjoined, and Chan's deferential approach was intrinsic to the realization of Okashimo's 'experiential' masterplan for the entire site. As befits a place that is effectively a stage set for contemplation and environmental reciprocity, Okashimo choreographed a promenade determined by the panorama, whereby a process of concealment and subsequent revealment begins at arrival. Rows of hedges, thickly leaved yang na trees, and the living pavilions are used to hide the views to the mountain on descent from above, before all (or nearly all) is revealed at the base, on the pool deck. But even then, the vista is partly occluded – the mountain is not presented in its naked glory, it remains veiled by artfully positioned trees with gently fluttering leaves. One is left with an impression, and a somewhat enigmatic one at that, rather than a perfectly realized moment. Which is also the way that one is left feeling about the place itself – one's mind has been both challenged and rested.

ABOVE The view to the sacred mountain, Doi Luang Chiang Dao, is only revealed on the pool deck at the lowest level of the retreat.

ABOVE Tucked away beneath wide-spreading eaves and black-stained ceilings, the interior spaces feel as if they are embedded in the earth. **OVERLEAF** Looking down from the entry to the compound. The roofs of the pavilions are covered with trumpet vines.

OLIVE HOUSE

2018
SINGAPORE
GUZ ARCHITECTS

The houses of Guz Wilkinson have slowly but surely defined much of the landscape, and indeed the image, of Singapore's leafy and affluent areas – those where stand-alone villas are officially termed Good Class Bungalows. Wilkinson set up practice in 1996 as an Arts and Crafts afficionado, determined to transplant and adapt the stylings of Voysey and Lutyens to the tropics, which was not entirely far-fetched – wide eaves, thick walls and integration with the landscape are actually very well-suited to the climate. In retrospect, he did signal something of a rejection of, or at least provide an alternative to, the strict orthogonality that was prevalent in Singapore at that time, but it was to take ten years before he hit upon a synthesis of predilections that transformed his architecture from homage to a most singular expression. With a collection of quite remarkable houses completed between 2008 and 2010, Wilkinson arranged every element of his architecture and his landscape as part of a clearly legible three-dimensional composition that proffered an equation between natural beauty, environmental reciprocity and luxuriant lifestyle. It was a formulation that updated the ethos (if not the fervour) of the Arts and Crafts movement for the twenty-first century, and he has conducted variations on that theme ever since.

With four pavilions linked on two levels around a water courtyard, Olive House occupies a sizable site at the top of a small rise, where it can pick up the slightest breezes, which then pass through the completely open living spaces on the ground floor. So far as is possible in Singapore, where the weather can lie heavy and insufferably hot, the house performs as a machine for passive ventilation. The swimming pool, to the immediate west of the house, and the courtyard ponds are only separated by the floor of the dining area, and the water surfaces thus generate further air movement. Those breezes are signified most refreshingly by a constant rustle from the leaves of the weeping tea trees that droop and sway from islands in the ponds, and which merge most delicately with the arrayed banks of phyllanthus that Wilkinson always uses to soften and camouflage the hard edges of the roof gardens. Accessible from every bedroom, the roof gardens feel as though they are on the ground floor, as part of an enveloping site-wide landscape, and through the processes of transpiration all that adjoining greenery cools the rooms still further. Wilkinson is matter of fact in regard to passive design in the tropics. 'It's so easy. It's so simple. You just need cross-ventilation,

LEFT View from the west, looking over the swimming pool to the layering of pavilions, courtyards and gardens.

overhangs, plants and water bodies. You can attribute that to learning from the vernacular, but really...it's just common sense.'

Evidently, Wilkinson considers the landscape to be as important as the architecture, and in a purely philosophical (sustainability-driven) sense, he would contend that landscape and the natural environment are all that matters. As he designs all his landscapes and gardens, he could be categorized and reviewed as a landscape architect. Yet his architecture has an especially strong and very distinctive formal quality, characterized by broad sweeping rooflines, smoothly crafted timber joinery and elegant metalwork. The proportions are horizontally inclined, and the scale is deceptively recessive – behind and beneath all that greenery, there lurks a classical rigour and rhythm that brings order to the craft and occasional whimsy.

Wilkinson's temperament and outlook have been very much conditioned by his years spent sailing, with many single-handed ocean voyages, and the means by which he intends his houses to operate are unmistakably informed by the mechanical and structural calibrations of a yacht. The wind is harnessed, the elements are held at bay and the power of passive energy delivers a primal sense of satisfaction.

ABOVE AND RIGHT Breezes flow continually above the water bodies and through the open spaces. Roof gardens are layered as extensions to the bedrooms. **OVERLEAF** Dotted with tree-filled islands, the internal water courtyard is surrounded by open living spaces. Black steel trellises screen direct sunlight.

MALCOMSON-CLAYTON HOUSE

2003
SINGAPORE
JOHN HEAH

John Heah is best known for the Four Seasons Sayan (completed in 1998), which marked a rather radical and somewhat controversial turning point in Balinese resort design, not so much for its architectural innovation as for its supposed lack of adherence to traditional forms. Up to that point, Balinese resort architecture had been directed by a desire to provide an appearance and an experience of authenticity, which was in itself slightly problematic, as luxury hotels have never been a traditional building type. Heah instead took a metaphorical approach, likening the hotel's very visible elliptical profile to a rice bowl, which, when filled with water on its roof, could be seen as a Balinese Hindu welcome gesture. As it transpired, however, the real legacy of the design was in Heah's consummate blending of exterior and interior materials and form. The architecture was very rich, indeed powerful, in a tectonic sense – it was clearly articulated and charmingly proportioned, and it exuded an eclectic yet culturally appropriate sensibility.

Designed shortly thereafter, Malcomson-Clayton House reaffirmed Heah's richness of expression. Both internally and externally, the architecture was intricate yet sumptuous, referencing a variety of materials, textures, styles and construction methods. As with the Sayan resort, the house was set on a steep slope, and it appears from the street as a discreet and well-mannered single-storey villa. Upon entry, however, the immediate vista is of opulence, as the site falls away as an Escher-like three-storey void, embellished by the ornate timber fretwork of the balustrades, staircases, decks and viewing platforms, and the central lift-well. That lift-well serves as a visual pivot for the entire composition, which takes up a C-plan (with a small hook to the left) that almost completely wraps around a levelled courtyard with gardens and pools at the base of the sunken site. The façades looking over the courtyard have an imperious expression, with heavily timbered enclosed verandahs that call to mind those of southern

OPPOSITE On a site that falls sharply to the east, the street-level entry is on the top floor of a circulation volume centred by a lift well. **ABOVE** The over-scaled and rhythmically tapered downpipes are built from black granite.

Spain and Italy as much as they do Malaysia and Indonesia. (The architect was in fact directly referencing the shutters and panels of the corridors and bedrooms of the Cheong Fatt Tze Mansion in Penang.) The timber joinery is exquisitely detailed, and its ornamentation is extended and enhanced by the use of stonework and masonry: the rhythmically tapered downpipes are made from black granite; pale stone is used throughout the pool area and the undercroft beneath the far bedroom; and the slender, gracefully vaulted trusses of the living rooms are formed of concrete.

The almost delicate integration of concrete echoes the tectonic dexterity displayed at the Sayan resort, where the avowedly vernacular stylings had something of a 'Lautneresque' futuristic appearance. The formidable concrete massing was leavened by walls and flooring of pale granite, while here in Singapore, the resplendence of the timber joinery – the cabinetwork – is leavened by the subservience of the concrete, of its skeletal structural elements. The atrium of the entry foyer has a grand, monumental scale, with a roof of coffered skylights and a reflection pool at the base, which contains three huge tribal drums from Borneo, arrayed as if intrinsic components of the architectural parti.

This compound effectively serves as a mini resort, which has been one of the prime motivations for high-end tropical house design over the last few decades, but its overall disposition is palatial rather than domestic. Heah was not yielding to any social or cultural context other than the immediate. This was an artful virtuoso piece of architecture that never strayed into the territory of undisciplined and untoward self-indulgence, and it must be remarked that in its complexity, its harmony and its tectonic inventiveness, we have rarely seen its like again.

ABOVE Looking into the courtyard garden from the base of the western circulation volume.

ABOVE The downstairs living room is roofed by gently curving concrete trusses. **OPPOSITE** A poolside undercroft displays the rich and varied use of materials, with concrete trusses, pale stone walls and crafted timber joinery.

OPPOSITE Looking down from the entry level to the circulation volume, which houses an Escher-like sequence of timber stairways, balustrades and walkways.

ABOVE Tribal drums from Borneo sit at the base of the three-level atrium, while coffered skylights provide soft illumination on the top floor.

ABOVE A completely open living space and viewing platform on the ground floor looks west toward the mountains and sea.

TELEGRAPH POLE HOUSE

2009
PULAU LANGKAWI, MALAYSIA
BUILDING BLOC ARCHITECTS

'Bob and Angela asked us to build a timber house because they had fallen in love with traditional Malay houses. However, we felt there was a high ecological cost, that building a house with new timber would be completely unsustainable, and we would also need to deal with the inherent construction problems of shrinkage and warping,' explain the architects, continuing, 'All over Malaysia, the old timber utility poles were being replaced by concrete poles, and we were thinking that the disused poles could make very beautiful columns, as they had a wonderful greyish weathered patina that only comes with time.'

Wen Hsia and BC Ang, wife and husband, and self-proclaimed blue-collar architects – 'no background, no pedigree...no design philosophy and no sound-clever flowery language'[1] – were commissioned in 2007 by an English couple to build their retirement villa on the island of Langkawi. At that time, a new generation of Malaysian architects was gaining attention across the region for works that intertwined the use of cheap and cast-off materials with a refined design sensibility. On the one hand, the architecture was conducive to very comfortable occupation; on the other hand, it was embedded in and emblematic of local culture, history and society. Along with Kevin Low (see p. 278) and Ng Seksan (see p. 266), Hsia and Ang, then known as Building Bloc Architects[2], were very much part of that movement, as heralded by their own Number 11 House in Petaling Jaya. They also stated their intention for the house in Langkawi: 'We aspired to make cultural connections through indirect references, fusing tested practices of tradition and local crafts with contemporary techniques to achieve an architecture of collaboration.'

Sitting in isolation at the top of a small hill, surrounded by thick forest and reached by a rambling driveway, Telegraph Pole House has extensive views toward the sea in the west. Its ground floor comprises little more than an open space for relaxation, completely sheltered by the living areas above. That open space/viewing platform is, however, a place of architectonic delight, in both a modernist and traditional manner. The plan and section are resolutely rectangular, with a square grid of columns thrice repeated across a smoothly concreted floor. It was a clinically modernist structural parti, then rendered in vernacular style by the comprehensive use of recycled

ABOVE Perched high on a hillside and surrounded by jungle, the house is distinguished by a sweeping hipped roof, clad in recycled timber shingles.

hewn timber. The big idea, which underpinned the formalist yet traditional composition of the entire house, was to make the columns out of disused '5 × 5' utility poles, stockpiled in a timber yard in Alor Setar, northern Malaysia. Graphically adorned by power corporation markings, the poles were placed in clusters of four, as pilotis that pirouette on steel plates above a single pin. As load-bearing columns they combine elemental rigour with tactile delight – a sensibility that goes on to permeate the entire house.

Reached by a timber staircase suspended from steel rods, the second floor is wrapped by verandahs (or *serambi*, as they are referred to locally) with balustrades, also made from steel rods in a quasi-industrial touch that extends the underlying modernist rigour of the architecture. This upper level contains three ensuite bedrooms and a central living room sheltered beneath a pitched timber roof with a very wide spread, whose vernacular appearance belies the precision of its structural grid. The height of the roof stimulates sufficient fan-accelerated airflow to obviate any requirement for air-conditioning and the concomitant sealing of rooms, which would have simply despoiled the wonderful permeability and openness of the living spaces. The recycled telegraph poles from Alor Setar were used for the framework of the roof, which was surfaced by shingles of belian wood (Borneo ironwood) retrieved from a superannuated hotel in Penang. The timber used for the walls and floors was likewise salvaged from a jetty, also in Penang. Crowned by the soaring proportions of the great wooden roof, the bedrooms have an undeniably palatial quality, albeit with a suitably rustic ambience, embellished by antique furnishings that share the gently faded patina of the recycled timber surfaces.

The no-frills and cost-conscious approach of Hsia and Ang conspired, ironically, to deliver a house that was quickly and widely hailed as something of a landmark in luxury tropical lifestyle. The lesson here then, the moral of the story, is that luxury really constitutes nothing more than the immediate gratification of the senses, and, in an architectural sense, that means doing the right thing – contextually, environmentally and climatically. As the architects point out, their motivations were ecological and cultural, and thus, by extension, their ethical position was uncompromised: 'The design sought to embody the spirit of the traditional Malay house in response to the tropical climate and the history of woodworking craft. The fundamental principles of the Malay houses – cross-ventilated, raised on stilts, shaded by large verandahs with sweeping roof overhangs, and built from low-thermal timber – were faithfully applied.'

ABOVE Steel rods are used for balustrades and railings, adding a quasi-industrial touch and reinforcing the underlying modernist rigour of the architecture.

ABOVE The columns are made from disused utility poles, sourced from a timber yard in Alor Setah, northern Malaysia.

TOP The utility poles are placed on a grid in clusters of four, resting on steel plates above a single pin. **ABOVE AND OVERLEAF** The upper-level living areas are sheltered and cross-ventilated beneath a pitched timber roof with a very broad spread.

SINURAMBI

2004
PENAMPANG, SABAH, MALAYSIA
FAHSHING ARCHITECT

Sinurambi is one of those houses that you expect to see a lot more of in Southeast Asia, but hardly ever do: a contemporary, very literal tribute to local vernacular that is both thoughtful and celebratory. Ling Fahshing grew up in Kota Kinabalu, the largest town in the territory of Sabah on the island of Borneo, and graduated as an architect from Arizona State University in 1985. He worked in the USA before returning to Sabah in 1990 and setting up his own practice in 2001, when he was commissioned by the English expatriate couple Terry and Rose Mills to design their 'dream home' in Penampang, high in the foothills of Mount Kinabalu. (It is interesting to note that two of the most traditionally inflected and contextually aware recent hideaway houses in the region – the other being Telegraph Pole House in Langkawi, see p. 176 – had English expatriates as clients.) Perched on a spur above the rainforest at 300 metres (1,000 feet) above sea level, the site was spectacular, with panoramic views to the ocean to the west and Mount Kinabalu to the northeast. *Sinurambi* means 'jungle hut' in the local Kadazan language, and Fahshing set out to 'grow a house as a natural occurrence of the jungle...we should go on a sort of "green offensive" and create conditions that propagate lifeforms in and around our habitat.'

The house sits in splendid isolation, and when glimpsed from a distance it has a rather majestic and romantic presence, rising above the all-enveloping swathes of jungle, not exactly as a hut but as a tribal command post or gathering place. The overall volume, which angles around the southeast entry courtyard on an L-shaped plan, has three components with disparate expressions: a living area to the south, a central circulation tower and the northern bedroom wing. The living area is contained within an octagonal framework of timber trellises and slender angled trusses, which are sheltered by a fanning canopy of plywood-lined eaves. The expression of this pavilion takes its cues from local vernacular construction, from the longhouses of the Kadazan people of the Penampang region in particular, where a distinctive profile was created by the outward-sloping walls of the above-ground communal areas. The longhouse walls are effectively bamboo screens, which ventilate the interior spaces, and are in turn protected by the overhanging thatched roofs. The compositional elements of Sinurambi mimic the oblique forms of this environmentally directed construction, as well referencing the outwardly flaring proportions of the *wakid*, a Kadazan basket. As an

LEFT Adjoined by a glazed stairway tower, the living areas at left are contained within an octagonal framework of timber trellises and angled trusses. **ABOVE** The house sits in splendid isolation, rising above the all-enveloping jungle of Mount Kinabalu's foothills.

ABOVE AND OPPOSITE BOTTOM LEFT The western elevation is composed of plywood wall panels, timber structural elements and black steel columns.

ordered architectural language, this expression is continued along the length of the western elevation, where a sequence of plywood wall panels and stained-timber structural members is punctuated by the black steel columns supporting the central stairway volume.

The architecture of the intermediary circulation volume has a more eclectic use of materials, and Fahshing was intent upon referencing and directly interacting with the house's immediate natural surroundings. The main eastern entry is framed by rubble walls made of sandstone quarried on the site, which then extend through the interior spaces, while the outdoor decks and balconies are built from selangan batu, a local hardwood. A cylindrical glazed atrium, capped on high by a pitched roof, encloses a stairwell with an organic spiral form inspired directly by the coiling ferns (paku pakis) that grow profusely in the vicinity. Fahshing, who passed away in 2011, was entranced by the relationship between construction and nature, and, ipso facto, by the fundamental virtues of organic architecture: 'This is an attempt to reveal the forms and approaches in architecture that already exist in nature. Through a gradual but continuous effort, we will rediscover that architecture is a function of nature, it is not a tool to be used by us to overcome nature.'

TOP The flaring profile of the southern living area references the proportion of the longhouses of the Kadazan people, as well as the shape of their basketware.

ABOVE Rising through a cylindrical glazed atrium in the centre of the house, a spiral staircase was inspired by the coiling ferns found in the area.

ABOVE The entry to the main house has a palatial inflection, with walls of stacked granite, a stepped plinth and an extended canopy.

ordered architectural language, this expression is continued along the length of the western elevation, where a sequence of plywood wall panels and stained-timber structural members is punctuated by the black steel columns supporting the central stairway volume.

The architecture of the intermediary circulation volume has a more eclectic use of materials, and Fahshing was intent upon referencing and directly interacting with the house's immediate natural surroundings. The main eastern entry is framed by rubble walls made of sandstone quarried on the site, which then extend through the interior spaces, while the outdoor decks and balconies are built from selangan batu, a local hardwood. A cylindrical glazed atrium, capped on high by a pitched roof, encloses a stairwell with an organic spiral form inspired directly by the coiling ferns (paku pakis) that grow profusely in the vicinity. Fahshing, who passed away in 2011, was entranced by the relationship between construction and nature, and, ipso facto, by the fundamental virtues of organic architecture: 'This is an attempt to reveal the forms and approaches in architecture that already exist in nature. Through a gradual but continuous effort, we will rediscover that architecture is a function of nature, it is not a tool to be used by us to overcome nature.'

TOP The flaring profile of the southern living area references the proportion of the longhouses of the Kadazan people, as well as the shape of their basketware.

ABOVE Rising through a cylindrical glazed atrium in the centre of the house, a spiral staircase was inspired by the coiling ferns found in the area.

NASSIM ROAD HOUSES

2008
SINGAPORE
ERNESTO BEDMAR ARCHITECTS

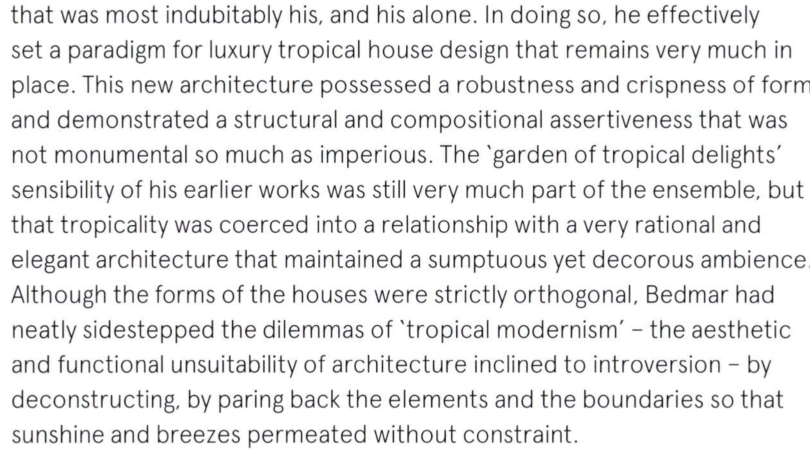

After establishing a reputation as an architect who judiciously blends a variety of tropical resort stylings with a deft touch and an eye for scenographic delight, Ernesto Bedmar hit upon a rich vein of work in the early 2000s that was most indubitably his, and his alone. In doing so, he effectively set a paradigm for luxury tropical house design that remains very much in place. This new architecture possessed a robustness and crispness of form, and demonstrated a structural and compositional assertiveness that was not monumental so much as imperious. The 'garden of tropical delights' sensibility of his earlier works was still very much part of the ensemble, but that tropicality was coerced into a relationship with a very rational and elegant architecture that maintained a sumptuous yet decorous ambience. Although the forms of the houses were strictly orthogonal, Bedmar had neatly sidestepped the dilemmas of 'tropical modernism' – the aesthetic and functional unsuitability of architecture inclined to introversion – by deconstructing, by paring back the elements and the boundaries so that sunshine and breezes permeated without constraint.

The Nassim Road Houses, built as a diptych across the road from each other in a secluded neighbourhood, stand as an especially clean and clear expression of Bedmar's formal program and, most notably, of his singular tectonic approach. Timber, steel, stone and masonry are combined and juxtaposed to play off each other, both in detail and at the scale of elevation. The main family house is reached by a twisting drive up a small hill, and its tiered elevation provides quite an exposé of the structural and material composition. Stone walls lie beneath a slender cantilevered layering of balconies and a floating roof; timber soffits and skylights bring in warmth and sunshine; and the tripartite section of the house is graphically revealed – the service zones, circulation areas and living spaces are separated by high blade walls. Facing on to a lawn enclosed by fully grown trees and high vine-clad retaining walls, this family house has a quiet sense of containment, with all rooms shielded by folding and sliding sets of screens. The white-painted central circulation volume has a relatively demure, abstracted expression, which is constantly enlivened by the striations of sunlight passing through battened screens and skylights.

The entry sequences for both houses have a beautifully composed palatial inflection, with low flights of steps, walls of smooth-edged pieces of layered

LEFT The eastern elevation of the main family home provides a graphic expression of Ernesto Bedmar's structural and material arrangements.

ABOVE The entry to the main house has a palatial inflection, with walls of stacked granite, a stepped plinth and an extended canopy.

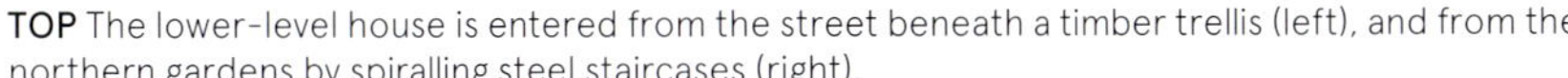

TOP The lower-level house is entered from the street beneath a timber trellis (left), and from the northern gardens by spiralling steel staircases (right).

ABOVE The garden elevations of the main house (left) and a small guesthouse (right) are enclosed by sliding and folding timber screens.

granite, and hovering filigreed canopies. The lower-level house was built for family recreation and guest accommodation, and it takes the form of a pavilion – quite literally, as it adjoins a tennis court. Its exposed northern elevation is something of a Bedmar set piece, with a classical rhythmic arrangement of granite piers, timber screens, slender columns, a thin skillion roof, a long reflection pool and a set of spiralling steel staircases. The open-plan living and dining areas on the upper floor are bathed in sunshine dappled through slender strips of timber, and, looking out to a lush surrounding landscape, the vista is that of tropical space-making at its most elemental and luxurious.

Bedmar's dexterous manipulations of space and mass were derived from his realization that in the tropics 'only the roof and columns are essential', and all else can be arranged and assembled almost by choice to enhance the delectations of occupation. His consequent achievement, the conflation of sybaritic pleasure with refined aesthetic expression, is quite apparent to those who have had the luck or wherewithal to experience the architecture. However, in purely formal terms, the fundamentals of Bedmar's architecture could have further applications, beyond the self-referential context of the luxury house. He has been an exceptionally innovative architect, and his designs, when stripped back to their bare bones, must be regarded as prototypes for tropical construction at a public scale as well as domestic.

ABOVE The airy circulation volume of the main house is slotted between the living areas and the service zones.

OPPOSITE RIGHT AND ABOVE A variety of spaces in both houses are lit from above, with sunlight spilling through trellises with slender timber battens.

WALLS AND ROOFS – MORE OR LESS

`Only the roof and columns are essential…we can live without the rest.´ ERNESTO BEDMAR[1]

As a distinctive entity, tropical architecture could only be categorized as such after a 'declaration of independence' had been unknowingly signed sometime in the 1980s.[2] As the nations of tropical Asia had shaken off the shackles of empire in the aftermath of the First World War, so too did their architects, but a 'post-colonial' dilemma, or tension, was equally as hard to escape. The first waves of architects who came to prominence had generally been trained in the West, and when it came to designing houses for a warm climate, the prescribed templates were fundamentally those of post-war Los Angeles – the works of John Lautner, Richard Neutra and Craig Ellwood, the Case Study Houses, and the all-pervading influence of Frank Lloyd Wright.

The problem was, of course, that Los Angeles is in the temperate zone, and however much Asian architects wished, or felt obliged, to implement the essential formulation, they were confounded by the exigencies of the tropics – the year-long heat, the blinding rainfalls, the invasive vegetation and the spifflicating humidity. Yet, as elsewhere across the world, the planning principles and lifestyle attributes of the California template remain regionally entrenched – the free and easy flow between inside and outside relationship is just too appealing – and contemporary house design can be dissected as an amalgam of the imported modern and the traditional local. There is, however, a critical difference between the principles and techniques of tropical vernacular construction and those of American suburbia, and it is purely elemental – it concerns walls, or the lack of them, and how they should be erected, arranged and operated. The structure of the walls and, ipso facto, the roof above, is key to the processes of tropical house design, even if as Ernesto Bedmar suggests, you only need columns.

Whether inspired by curiosity, environmental awareness, a reverence for traditional methods, or financial necessity, architects throughout the region have been conspicuously inventive in the fabrication of walls – many of which, unsurprisingly, have been for their own houses. Boonserm Premthada, of Bangkok Project Studio (see p. 272), is noted for his innovations in construction materials, and built his family house using pale-grey bricks made from fly ash, mixed with cement and sand. As the sizes of the handmade bricks were somewhat wayward, a creamy mortar was used to level the layers, and it blurts out from the cracks as a signifier of the architecturally untoward and experimental. Premthada's compatriot, Boonlert Hemvijitraphran of Boon Design (see p. 234), was motivated by the desire to make his new house look 'old from the start', and his arrays of screens and windows have an external expression and colouration that most deliberately recall those of traditional

ABOVE Boon Design, Aurapin House, Bangkok, Thailand, 2004.

ABOVE Wallmakers, Nisarga, Angamaly, India, 2023.

Thai houses built from teak. He was, however, building his 'walls' from steel and glass. Vinu Daniel, based in Trivandrum, has devised various methods for making walls from recycled materials, and refuses to countenance other means of construction (his practice is actually named Wallmakers; see p. 228). He regularly engages in a process that he refers to as a 'shuttered debris wall technique', wherein the walls of the houses are built from whatever waste material can be tracked down and salvaged in local scrapyards, then compounded and mixed with sand, soil and cement.

Rajasthan is renowned, almost glorified, for its monuments built from stone over the ages – the fabled forts, palaces and stepwells, and the wonderfully decorous Hawa Mahal. However, as Malik Architecture points out, the local sandstone is now only considered as material for cladding and is seldom used for its inherently sustainable structural properties. As per the monumental edifices of yesteryear, Stone House in Jaipur was constructed with load-bearing sandstone walls, but they are not solid (see p. 238). The walls have hollow cavities, which serve as a thermal break, one where the heat soaked up by the external surfaces is released before affecting the spaces within. The internal temperatures were effectively decreased by 6°C, in a city where the average reading in summer hovers around 40°C.

Suresh, an engineer who worked with Laurie Baker in Trivandrum for many years and commissioned his final house, recalls that Baker was supremely knowledgeable in every aspect, whether it be construction, engineering, spatial relationships, material usage, and the local climatic and environmental conditions. Beginning with his early work for leprosy missions across India, Baker had long been a devoted practitioner of what we would now describe as 'sustainable architectural practice', and his construction methods and design philosophy have had considerable and wide-ranging influence.[3] He stressed that he learnt pretty much all he knew from his studies of vernacular construction, realizing that – given the limited available finance and range of materials – he would have little option but to reapply the attributes of local techniques and craftsmanship. (It might also be noted that his friend, Mahatma Gandhi, told him that all houses should be built with materials sourced within five miles of the site). Baker preferred to build in brick and masonry, including mud walls, and his structures were notable for their frugality, their idiosyncratic shapes and details, and, above all, their systems of environmental control, or passive design (in current parlance). Jali screens, air vents, wide ledges and eaves, water harvesting, orientation toward prevailing winds, the use of recycled and salvaged materials, and the retention of the natural environment, were all integral

TOP Malik Architecture, Stone House, Jaipur, India, 2019. **ABOVE** Lal Chand Ustad, Hawa Mahal, Jaipur, India, 1799.

to his work. Isavasyam, the house completed in 1998 for Suresh and his wife Neerada (see p. 206), afforded him a long-awaited opportunity to build over four levels with bricks laid in a rat-trap bonding system, which provided a three-inch cavity – a thermal buffer zone – that rose the full height of the load-bearing walls.[4]

For at least the first forty years of the post-Second World War era, the architecture of tropical Asia – essentially that of public building – was 'characterized' by the use of concrete, a trajectory reinforced by the monumental virtuosity of Le Corbusier's works at Chandigarh. By the latter stages of his career, Le Corbusier had been captivated by the robust sculptural qualities of off-form concrete, and, as passed down the line, its usage almost became emblematic of regional and national self-assertion. (The somewhat loose appellation of 'International Style' hints at the worldwide processes of post-colonial dissemination.) Off-form concrete possesses a certain distinctive charm in a hot and steamy environment, not least because of the organic discolourations of its weathering processes, and its usage now quite agreeably constitutes a 'genre' of tropical house design, one whose attributes are, curiously enough, those of tactility, softness and environmental deference. John Bulcock of Design Unit, based in Kuala Lumpur (see p. 200), has designed several houses in this vein, and revels in its appearance: 'As the concrete is left unfinished when the formwork is removed, the slightly rough and organic surfaces look beautiful in the changing sunlight.' His architecture is elementally directed not so much by the walls as by the roofs, which 'float' as insulating concrete parasols above interlinking sets of permeable cross-ventilated rooms, where continuous strips of clerestory windows – slotted between the roofs and sequences of ring beams – have become a signature of his architecture. The application of off-form concrete by the Indonesian architect, Andra Matin (see p. 256), is far more comprehensive and imperious – walls are rendered in their entirety as blank grey canvases – but the overall effect is strangely recessive, almost as if a phenomenological trick has been played, one in which the natural environment has claimed the edifices as its own.

ABOVE Laurie Baker, Isavasyam, Trivandrum, India, 1998.

ABOVE Design Unit, Dama zAmya, Phuket, Thailand, 2010.

'You need architecture without walls, but you also need protection from rain, so you need walls that can float away.' JIMMY LIM

ABOVE Vo Trong Nghia Architects, Ha Long Villa, Ha Long, Vietnam, 2020.

ABOVE WOHA, Singapore Pavilion, Expo 2020, Dubai.

Vo Trong Nghia, of VTN Architects (see p. 222), has designed a variety of multi-level houses and small commercial projects in Vietnam that gladly welcome the colonization of nature. Built using perforated brickwork or off-form concrete, they were internally and externally landscaped with gardens on every level marked by a profusion of trees, and this horticultural integration was specifically directed by the architect's intention 'to include as much greenery as there was in the original landscape'. A similar strategy for rewilding had earlier been formalized by WOHA in the early 2000s (see p. 118), referring to their calculations as the Green Plot Ratio, and it was one of a range of proposals for evaluating a building's social and ecological performance.[5] At the Dubai Expo of 2020, WOHA unveiled a Singapore Pavilion that was devoid of external walls, and resembled nothing so much as a thoroughly 'greened' and herbaceous tropical house. Set in lavish gardens beneath a slender floating roof covered with solar panels, a series of conical semi-enclosed rooms rising over three levels was consummately 'carpeted' by walls of flowering plants.

In Huế, central Vietnam, all that you can see from the outside of the Labri House – and all that you can look into from the inside – is greenery (see p. 218). Consisting of nothing more than four interlocking cubic volumes with completely transparent walls of glass, it is literally a greenhouse – insulated, screened and protected by trees, creepers, vines and shrubs, and by frangipanis planted on the roofs. The architect, Nguyen Khai, amiably observes that birds, butterflies and the weaving vines are as much at home as the human occupants, and he likens the 'randomness' of the micro-environment to that of a tree. As the structure is innocuous to the point of invisibility, the architecture of the Labri House does not have an aesthetic per se – it is a geometric ordering and enclosure of natural conditions. However, as demonstrated by the deft compositions of Vo Trong Nghia, the creation of a 'green' aesthetic – rather than the (admittedly highly admirable) caging of the jungle – does require architectonic control, or it is a case of 'where's the architecture, what's the point?' At the scale of a house, unlike that of high-rise buildings, curtain walls of greenery do not flatter the architecture, all they do is hide it. The diaphanous and wispy 'gardens' that drift delicately from the ledges of Guz Wilkinson's houses are environmentally beneficial and lovely

ABOVE Wallflower Architecture + Design, Touching Eden House, Singapore, 2023.
OPPOSITE Nguyen Khai Architects & Associates, Labri House, Huê, Vietnam, 2021.

to behold, but the lyricism of the timber form-making still shines through (see p. 164). Likewise, the trails of creepers and the clusters of flowering plants that adorn the timber strips on the walls of Touching Eden House by Wallflower Architecture + Design (see p. 212), only focus one's attention when considered as part of an architectonic artwork.

The aesthetics of tropical architecture, whether green, grey, brown or a mottled somewhere in-between, are ultimately determined by the perpetual 'liveliness' of its environment. As Kevin Low says: 'My inspirations are driven by a response to the driving rains, and that sun which creates a remarkable rate of growth and decay that cakes everything.'

GREEN BRIDGE HOUSE

2017
KUALA LUMPUR, MALAYSIA
DESIGN UNIT

John Bulcock's arrival in Kuala Lumpur in late 1994 turned out to be the final stop for a peripatetic and idealistic young English architect. He had travelled widely, both as a student at Hull School of Architecture and as a graduate, meeting and occasionally working with several eminent architects, and spending much of his time 'drawing and taking notes'. While still a student in 1981, he worked for four months with Paolo Soleri on the Arcosanti project in Arizona, a utopian exercise in communal sustainability described by architectural critic Oliver Wainwright as, 'a revolutionary new model of super-dense urban living, a vast multi-levelled concrete megastructure that would house 5,000 people in self-sufficient harmony.'[1] Soleri had studied under Frank Lloyd Wright, and as Bulcock would later work in Ahmedabad with Balkrishna Doshi, who had assisted both Le Corbusier and Louis Kahn, he claims with some pride that, 'I consider that I have links to the three greatest architects of the 20th century'. It is not a great stretch to spot those links, those influences, in his completed architecture, along with (as he acknowledges) those of Doshi, Laurie Baker and Geoffrey Bawa. Bulcock's unwavering implementation of methods for sustainable construction might thus be appreciated as the continuation of a hot-climate architectonic lineage, one that might be regarded as a synthesis between modernist rigour, organic tactility and the inherent appropriateness of vernacular principles.

On settling in Kuala Lumpur, Bulcock worked for a year with Jimmy Lim and then for the Danish firm of Skaarup & Jespersen before setting up his own practice, Design Unit, in 2001. The early years of the twenty-first century were something of a febrile time in Malaysian architecture. In their highly individualistic and pioneering fashion, Jimmy Lim and Ken Yeang had been the spearheads of two dynamic expressions of tropical form-making, but they were ceding ground to the likes of Kevin Low, Ng Seksan, Wen Hsia and BC Ang, who had reverted to a more 'rootsy' approach, acknowledging and indeed revelling in the imperfections of modern urbanity. The work of Bulcock segued rather neatly with this new expression, quite clearly eschewing any tendency toward bravura and delighting in the interplay between architecture, landscape and context. However, 'neatly' underscores a critical differentiation – Bulcock's architecture is always tidy and fastidious. His use of off-form (fair-

LEFT Built from off-form concrete on a site that falls away from the street, the house encloses and overlooks a secluded private garden.

faced) concrete is neither rough nor polished, it is employed delicately and unobtrusively, and, as he points out, the intention is to 'emphasize the spaces rather than the materials themselves...architecture is about how we perceive space'.

Completed in 2017, Green Bridge House forms part of a sequence that began around ten years earlier with a collection of easily identifiable Design Unit houses, built mainly in Kuala Lumpur, with a couple of outliers in Phuket and Sri Lanka. They were each built with an off-form concrete framework that embraced or overlooked courtyard gardens, and which could be clearly read as 'machines for breathing', for providing constant ventilation and solar protection. Located in Bukit Gasing, a leafy and pleasant inner-suburban enclave of Kuala Lumpur, Green Bridge House appears as a discreet single-storey elevation from the street, perched on a site that falls away to the south to greet what Bulcock describes as 'a green wall of landscape' to the rear. The two-level house is duly arranged on a U-shape plan (with a small pavilion on the east) that encloses and overlooks a self-contained private landscape, which contains lawns, gardens and a swimming pool. The public living areas (to the west) and the private bedroom wings (to the north) are linked by a bridge – named Le Pont Vert in honour of the French owner – and all the circulation routes through the house are treated as inside/outside experiences, lit by striated sunlight passing through the slender beams above, or through a series of bamboo screens. Those screens are also used to filter sunlight entering the living areas, which are illuminated from on high by clerestory windows slotted between a set of ring beams and the roof.

The most dramatic space is the double-height living room. It is here where all the years of Bulcock's immersion in the delights and functional values of a certain sort of architecture are there to see. The compositional harmony, the combination of materials and the integration with nature have conspired to provide a veritable gallery for living. The ground-floor dining and relaxation areas are overlooked by the entry lobby, and by a mezzanine-level library whose fair-faced brick walls are aligned at angles to admit daylight while maintaining privacy. In conjunction with the mottled, softly stained appearance of the off-form concrete, and the gentle imprecisions of the bamboo screens, the unfinessed quality of the brickwork provides a tactile reiteration of the architecture that has long captivated John Bulcock. The organic, and the Arts and Crafts have once again permeated the systems for sustainable, functional and tasteful construction.

ABOVE View from the street entry, showing the slender overhead beams and the bridge between the living areas and the bedroom wing. **OPPOSITE** Looking down from the entry lobby to the gardens and pool below.

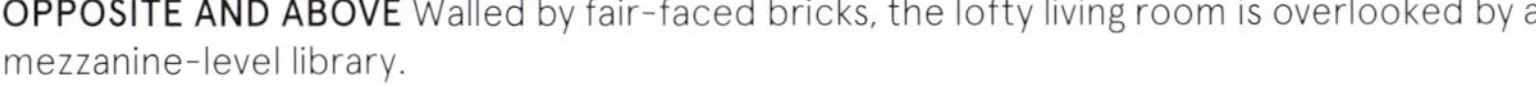

OPPOSITE AND ABOVE Walled by fair-faced bricks, the lofty living room is overlooked by a mezzanine-level library.

TOP Circulation routes are clad with bamboo screens. **ABOVE** Looking to the bedroom wing from the entry lobby.

ISAVASYAM

1998
TRIVANDRUM, INDIA
LAURIE BAKER

'People say my house is the quintessence of Laurie Baker, a kind of swansong. During summer break, I watched Mr Baker work. I'd wait for his morning visits. His cloth satchel slung over his shoulder, he gave instructions to the workers who all addressed him as Daddy,' explains Neerada Suresh. Neerada was married to Suresh in 1979, the year that Suresh, a civil engineer based in Trivandrum, began an intermittent professional relationship with Laurie Baker. Neerada, a poet and educator, recalls that she had her first sighting of Baker when waiting for a bus in the late 1960s – a friend pointed him out and said: 'Do you see that white guy there? He makes weird houses.' As she and Suresh got to know Baker well, she eventually and 'diffidently' asked whether he would design a home for them. He consented immediately, asked a range of questions, received his brief, and she did not hear back for five years. 'I thought he'd clean forgotten about me. Then on one of those evenings when your dream house is the last topic on your mind, I got a call from Mr Baker. He said he was ready to do my house.' With its meaning in Sanskrit as 'where God abides', Isavasyam was the last house that Baker designed and supervised before his death at the age of ninety.

Born and bred in Birmingham, UK, Laurie Baker graduated as an architect in 1937, first visiting India in 1943 en route home after being sent to China to work as an anaesthetist during the Second World War. He spent three months in Bombay, and became close friends with Mahatma Gandhi, with whom he discussed architecture at length: 'It was from the influence of Mahatma Gandhi I learnt that the real people you should be building for, and who are in need, are the ordinary people.' Gandhi also urged him to live and work in India, and he duly returned in 1945 and began designing leprosy missions across the country. In the 1960s, he settled in Trivandrum, in the southwestern state of Kerala, and proceeded – in the most humble and benevolent manner – to make his mark on the history of architecture and construction, leaving a localized legacy without compare. He was a supremely inventive and whimsical architect and craftsman, taking his cues from traditional techniques, and he was a committed environmentalist and a prophet for sustainability.

Suresh states: 'He was much more than just an architect. He was a master builder, he understood engineering, he understood the climate, and he simply knew everything about creating spaces and using materials.'

OPPOSITE The entry shows the lingering influence of the Arts and Crafts movement on Laurie Baker's work. **ABOVE** The roof is sculpted as 'one, big, coiled channel that delivers rainwater to a well beneath the garden'.

He continues by explaining the attributes of his own house:

> He had the idea of a helical coil, rising over four floors around a central courtyard. That means we have light from inside and outside. And the house is one big exhaust fan, with hot air escaping through circular venting chimneys, and with natural draughts entering through jali openings and windows. A two-foot overhang ensures that rainfall never hits the walls, and the roof is one big, coiled channel that delivers rainwater to a well beneath the garden.

As a consequence of Baker's innovations and material frugality, Suresh estimates that the house was built for one-third of the cost of a conventional construction, and, as he says, it was all done so that the house could breathe. Most significantly, the walls of the four-storey house were built with a rat-trap bonding system, whereby the bricks are placed vertically, not flat, thus creating a three-inch cavity that extends the full height of the structure. This produced a buffer zone for cooling and insulation, reduced the quantity of bricks needed, and the walls were able to bear all the loads required. Suresh had long been intrigued by Baker's use of rat-trap bond, and through his work with the Indian Housing and Urban Development Corporation, he commissioned a study in 1992 to assess its structural performance. The conclusion was that a rat-trap bonding system provided the strongest possible brick wall, and as Suresh observes, 'Baker already knew that, intuitively, but it had never been proved. Our house was the first time he went further than one storey.'

Aside from all that structural ingenuity, the experiential qualities are an absolute delight, with myriad internal spaces presenting a cornucopia of shapes, colours, grottos, artefacts, corbelled archways and patterned ceilings. An all-pervading sense of joyousness is overlaid with a hint of the spiritual – most notably in the lengthy curved living room, referred to as 'the cathedral' – and that conjunction can be traced back to the Arts and Crafts movement, and its abiding influence on all Baker's work.

Neerada's dream house had been built, and she recalls the legendary architect as a 'wonderful person, always cracking jokes and very friendly'. For his part, in one of his final interviews, Baker cheerfully described Neerada as the 'first client I've had who is as eccentric as I am'.

TOP The tall incisions in the rear elevation contain the stained-glass windows of the large, curved living room. **ABOVE** The ceilings are patterned with roof tiles and with circular venting chimneys that double as skylights with a basket-weave cap.

TOP AND OVERLEAF Wrapping around the internal courtyard, the grand elliptical living room is lit and ventilated on both sides. **ABOVE** A corbelled archway leads from the entry vestibule into the living room.

TOUCHING EDEN HOUSE

2023
SINGAPORE
WALLFLOWER ARCHITECTURE + DESIGN

Singapore is not blessed with sweeping views and wondrous topography – it is not exactly Rio de Janeiro or, come to that, even Kuala Lumpur – but it does have some very beautiful places. Despite the density and intensity of its urbanization, the island has retained an abundance of extremely liveable locations whose charms are those of the immediate natural environment. A large swathe of Singaporean suburbia has effectively remained inured to all the ongoing processes of modernization and remains a site for indulgence in what might be described as a tropical idyll, the house in paradise. And that paradise, that context, is purely botanic. The stately thickets of tall trees, the cascading plenitude of intermediate growth and the profusion of floral blooming – this is a Rousseau painting, a fantasy of benign tropicality come to life, and (for the most part) the villas of the affluent are content to recline within the languor. Some assertive architecture has been erected without contextual aforethought, and some vulgarities are rightly referred to as 'monster houses', but an ambience of too-good-to-be-true pervades on the gentle slopes of a vicinity where expensive houses are officially referred to as Good Class Bungalows.

Nestled into a low-lying site in a valley between two hillocks, Touching Eden House is, as the name suggests, about as close to paradise as you can get. You can almost reach out to touch the justly renowned Botanic Gardens from here – they are just across the road. As the architects say: 'The vision was to create an organic garden that coexists with Botanic Gardens. We wanted to craft a pavilion raised on stilts, wrapped in timber lattice and lush greenery.'

Wallflower Architecture + Design has established a formidable pedigree for a series of houses whose essential parti was clearly expressed: an open living area on the ground floor surmounted by a one-room-thick upper storey with a porous permeable façade. The breezes swirl through, the interior and exterior spaces are seamlessly connected, and there is little

LEFT AND ABOVE Looking toward the southern entry façade, showing the framework of timber strips crowned by flourishing foliage.

need for air-conditioning. The architecture of passive energy was clearly delineated, but Wallflower evolved a quite singular mode of tectonic expression, wherein the structure and the cladding were moulded with hints of mid-twentieth-century modernism, Mediterranean regionalism and Brazilian eloquence. The most unambiguous reference, however, was to the elevated colonial bungalow, whose ground floor effectively served as a sheltered courtyard. Those bungalows were of course influenced by and derived from vernacular structures, and a process of cross-pollination has been ongoing for centuries: the earlier colonial houses brought about a formalization of the kampung (village) house, whose traditional ornamentation and materials were then appropriated for modern construction, and so on. Wallflower's architecture thus forms a continuation of this process, blending a variety of influences in a distinctive fashion while not wavering from the essential correctness of the form.

In its appearance, Touching Eden House is not so immediately distinctive. If you glanced at it in passing, you would not readily identify it as a Wallflower house, which in terms of the architects' recent oeuvre is quite anomalous. This house was so subsumed by nature – and, ipso facto, by its context – that the as-accustomed legibility of expression was obscured, overtaken by the vision of an 'organic garden'. The appearance might have been different, but the parti remained intact, with a ground plane that extends through the long and narrow site without interruption – pool, lawn, gardens and living rooms occupy the one continuous space. The two upper storeys are enclosed by a façade of timber strips mounted on a steel frame, with vines and plantings tumbling in and out of the screens as vertical gardens, as an aesthetic extension of the Botanic Gardens and as an environmental filter. With the structural form hidden by the repetitive multiplicity of the timber elements (built from Accoya wood), the lengthy eastern elevation has an unexpectedly monumental dimension, resulting from the deceptive scale of the arrangement, where the timber strips resemble mullions on each of the seven layers of the external frame. Those layers then read as if a level, or a floor in a larger building, and, crowned by a projecting cornice and anchored by a grand opening at ground level, the façade then takes the image of a curtain-walled late International Style hotel or public building (the UNESCO headquarters in Paris springs to mind). Rather than a purely structural expression, the house can be seen as an architectonic artwork derived from its environmental function and from the sheer botanic delight of its location.

ABOVE Looking out to the eastern gardens from the open-plan living areas on the ground floor.

TOP Dappled sunlight pours into the house through steel frames, timber strips and trailing vines on the western elevation.

ABOVE At the southern tip of the house, the master bedroom is screened by trees and the random arrangement of timber slats. **OVERLEAF** The timber strips are layered as mullions along the length of the eastern elevation.

LABRI HOUSE

2021
HUẾ, VIETNAM
NGUYEN KHAI ARCHITECTS & ASSOCIATES

The diminutive Labri House is found in the beguilingly evocative environs of Huế's Imperial City, the palatial compound that served as Vietnam's centre of government during the reign of the Nguyen dynasty, and it takes no great leap of the imagination to perceive the ostensibly humble abode as a microcosm of that immediate context. Laid out in the early nineteenth century along the lines of the Forbidden City in Beijing, the central citadel and its landscape of ramparts, walls and lakes remains in place as a World Heritage Site, now fringed by the congestion and cacophony of urban Vietnam. Tucked away at the end of a narrow alley that leads off a busy road, the house occupies a small and very private plot on the eastern shore of one of the nine man-made lakes (lotus ponds in summer) that ring the Imperial City. In such a setting, its occupants can choose to either embrace or refrain from interaction with their surroundings – as was once done on the altogether grander scale of the citadel, where entry was forbidden to all but the imperial family.

Labri means a `secret place', a hideaway, and the design of this little house succumbs to the delights of seclusion as a point of first principle. The architecture was also impelled by the propinquity of the beautiful lake to engage unreservedly with the natural world. With a less than tangible sense of scale and proportion, the completed house is more of an apparition than an architectural object, sheathed by the minimal external structure of a conservatory. A slender white-painted steel framework supports sheer glass panels, and the dwelling resides within four completely transparent cubic volumes: a bathroom, a bedroom, a kitchen and a living/dining room. All the spaces – rooms and narrow external corridors – are screened by ceiling-to-floor trails of vines, which are actually referred

OPPOSITE The rooms and corridors comprise a sequence of micro-environments, an ephemeral and ever-changing organic live-in artwork. **ABOVE** The house is placed at the rear of a small plot of land that steps down to the waters of one of Huế's Imperial City lakes.

simplicity. He is fascinated by organic relationships rather than a need for expression:

> I let the architecture speak for itself. I wanted to open up all the spaces so that you would be immersed in greenery, so you are living in the plants and the trees. The core value was 'close to nature'. There are other creatures living inside this shelter, not just humans...there are birds and butterflies, and the vines weave into each other, making a green wall, for privacy and clean air. When you see the house, you might get the feeling that it has grown up randomly, as naturally as a tree coming out of the ground.

to by the architect as one of the three structural layers: glass, vines and concrete. The ambient dappled sunshine provides a quite naturally wonderful light source, while breezes flow constantly through an array of hinged glass doorways and vertical windows. The rooms and garden corridors coalesce as a continuous and apparently infinite sequence of micro-environments, which form a panorama, an ephemeral organic live-in artwork that is forever changing in accordance with the moods of the weather and the proliferations of the plants.

The house was placed to the high-walled rear of a previously unoccupied pocket of land, with the remainder of the site cultivated by the owners – a couple heading into retirement – as a vegetable garden stepping down to the lake. Supported by concrete columns and roof slabs concealed by greenery, fully grown frangipanis rise above each of the four blocks; and it must be noted that the logistical and structural requirements for tree relocation and installation formed the most complicated and demanding aspects of a building process that only took six months. The frangipanis on the roof were the architectural feature that mattered most.

Nguyen Khai is Huế born and bred, and he makes it clear that he is not preoccupied by the formality of architecture so much as a desire for

TOP AND ABOVE RIGHT The interior fittings have a compact modular arrangement that refrains from interfering with the ambience and outlook.

OPPOSITE Nguyen Khai refers to the three structural layers of the house as glass, vines and concrete.

HA LONG VILLA

2020
HA LONG, VIETNAM
VO TRONG NGHIA ARCHITECTS

The islands of Ha Long Bay present a memorable sight, with thousands of limestone pinnacles, forested cliff faces and tufted monoliths glimpsed in raggedy dreamlike arrays, as if in a scroll-painter's fantasy. It is a legendary location, one where the scenic merges with the mythic, and the landside shoreline has been built up recently as a town now focused more on tourism than its previous and rather less glamorous business of coalmining. The limestone karsts also rise above the streets of the city, and even though the architecture – the built environment – is decidedly prosaic, the landscape is imbued with the topographic otherworldliness.

Ha Long Villa, designed by Vo Trong Nghia (VTN) Architects, also rises above the streets, a few blocks back from the waterfront, as something of a topographical/geological fantasy, but its design impetus was not solely directed by a metaphorical allusion to its scenic context. The house is but one of several prototypes erected by the architects for their 'House for Trees' series of residential projects, which is explained as 'aiming to bring green spaces back into the city, and to include as much greenery as there was in the original [untouched] landscape to provide a healthier life for people living in the city. Due to the simplicity of the concept, the idea of "House for Trees" can be multiplied almost anywhere in tropical climate regions.'

Vo Trong Nghia is a very high-minded and highly principled practitioner, and it is illuminating to view his philosophy and his built works in the light of Vietnam's recent geopolitical emergence and, of course, its years of calamitous warfare. Born in 1976, shortly after the war ended, Nghia grew up in a village close to what had been the fiercely demarcated border between

OPPOSITE AND ABOVE The outer shell of the five-storey house appears as a rocky outcrop, complete with cave-like openings and studded with plants and trees.

north and south. He went on to study architecture at Hanoi University before winning a scholarship to Japan, where he studied intensively for ten years, gaining a Masters degree and a Ph.D. Upon his return to Vietnam, he set up his own practice in 2006, and he did not flinch from immediately implementing his principles. He was committed to green architecture, and he built and financed his first two projects as cafés, which displayed his ecological agenda and provided income for his nascent practice. 'My architecture was very different. My structures had a very beautiful quality of space, and they were inexpensive to build. But first, I had to prove to my potential clients that I could build such structures.'

As he became increasingly well-known, and his designs were featured extensively in the international journals, Nghia articulated his architectural intentions and social rationale in a manner that was both ingenuous yet very world aware. He recounts: 'My inspirations are very direct. I love trees and forests. I love the idea of living under a tree. I want to create buildings that allow us to live inside nature.' In a 2019 interview with *The New York Times*, he stated: 'Because there had been so much war, we were not able to develop a modern tradition of architecture in Vietnam. I wanted to create a kind of architecture that harmonized with nature, that did not need air-conditioning, that employed simple and cheap materials. I wanted to create a new language of architecture in our country.'[1] It would be too much to declare that Nghia was a revolutionary, or even a visionary, but when seen in the context of Vietnam's (and tropical Asia's) almost frightening rate of modernization and urbanization, what has distinguished his architecture is its originality: its conspicuous conjunction of experimental construction and expressive form-making with an abundance of greenery. From the outset, Nghia's objectives for sustainable design were directly derived from his attachment to vernacular construction and a traditional way of living,

ABOVE The mystical islands of Ha Long Bay are viewed from an external walkway: a vertical promenade that spirals up the full height of the house.

OPPOSITE The walkway functions as a buffer zone that protects and shields the interiors from heat and noise.

OPPOSITE AND ABOVE The off-form concrete structure is forcefully articulated, providing a counterpoint to the profusion of plants and trees.

and they were delightfully inflected by a very singular (almost childlike) form of romanticism.

The outer shell of Ha Long Villa appears as a rocky outcrop, complete with cave-like openings and studded with flourishing plants and trees at every level. That outer wall has a pentagonal plan, and it encloses another pentagon, separated by a buffer zone that serves as a walkway spiralling up around the five levels of the house, and, crucially, as a massive form of insulation and protection from heat and noise. The circuitous journey from the ground floor gardens to those on the roof is an architectural promenade of the first order, where one passes by trees and small gardens while gazing out at the vista of Ha Long Bay and above to the skies through an irregular sequence of boldly hewn cut-outs. Although playing second fiddle to the exuberance of the external composition and landscaping, the central interior volumes are forcefully articulated as a very non-organic – late period Le Corbusier – counterpoint to all that greenery, while functioning as a void for stack ventilation.

Ultimately, the abiding image of the structure is that of an overgrown ruin, an abandoned house, one where nature has taken over and re-colonized a man-made geological edifice. And one might be tempted to believe that such a scenario does not diverge too far from the architect's outlook.

NISARGA

2023
ANGAMALY, INDIA
WALLMAKERS

Lakshmi and Vishnu are musicians with two young children, and when they set about building a house for themselves on a parcel of land in central Kerala that belonged to Vishnu's family, they researched online to find an architect who was eco-friendly and had a knowledge of mud-wall construction. They quickly alighted upon Vinu Daniel. Daniel graduated as an architect from Trivandrum's College of Engineering in 2005, and, after working for a couple of years with the Auroville Earth Institute on post-tsunami reconstruction in the Pondicherry region, he set up his own practice back in Trivandrum. As his first project comprised little more than an artfully designed wall, the practice was duly christened Wallmakers. With an avowed commitment to 'sustainable and cost-effective architecture', the practice soon began to make quite a name for itself, going on to win a slew of local and international awards. Daniel speaks fervently about the current responsibilities of architecture, pointing to the elephant in the room of contemporary construction:

> In the global climate crisis, it becomes all-the-more important to question the direction in which we humans are headed. In place of questions like 'What should we build?', we need to be asking, 'Should we build?' As it is inevitable that we must build, we need to use materials that are not new...we should only use materials that have been used before.

The plot of land was roughly 40 kilometres (25 miles) to the northeast of Kochi in the district of Angamaly, which has a wondrously languid and bucolic landscape, with winding roads and fields dotted with charming bungalows. When Daniel visited the site, he was 'very inspired' recalls Lakshmi, finding the view over a paddy field to the east to be particularly appealing. Observing that the predominant feature of the local built environment was the traditional Kerala tiled roof, Daniel suggested that the house should quite simply be surmounted by one of those pitched roofs and open out to that vista. The essential problem of the Kerala roof, however, is that despite its virtues – solar insulation, rain protection and contextual harmony – the interior spaces get very dark. As Lakshmi and Vishnu also wanted their new house to serve as a rehearsal and performance venue, Daniel came up with the idea of illuminating the interiors with skylights that could also function as rooftop seating for

OPPOSITE Skylights in the south-facing roof can be used as seating for outdoor performances when a stage is laid over the swimming pool. **ABOVE** The northwest entry elevation displays the triangular geometry that continues throughout the house, both in plan and section.

an outdoor amphitheatre. (A temporary stage is quickly assembled by laying planks over a swimming pool at the southern base of the roof's slope.)

The triangular pitch of the roof was then a progenitor for the site plan, wherein the house itself was laid out upon an isosceles right-angled triangle,[1] with the northwest entry façade as the longest elevation. Each of the internal spaces were then symmetrically disposed on triangular plans, as an open-plan living room, a kitchen, a recording studio, and bedrooms and bathrooms. The timber-floored living and dining area also serves as a performance space, and the furniture arrangements are extremely flexible, with sunken 'trenches' for the legs and feet of those sitting on the floor, and triangular tables that can be variously configured. The load-bearing walls were built from Daniel's 'shuttered debris wall technique', and are composed of all sorts of debris salvaged from neighbouring towns and mixed with soil collected on site. A set of metal racks discovered in a scrapyard are used as frames to support screens of creepers outside the bedroom windows, and most of the furniture and artefacts were also reconditioned and repurposed. Hot air can escape through vents in the roof, and the ceilings are lined with jute sacking, which bathes the interiors in a lovely soft wash of daylight.

Such a degree of technical inventiveness in the name of sustainable construction has distinguished Wallmakers as flagbearers for a generation of ecologically minded architects[2] – one that would undoubtedly query whether any other type of practitioner could now have validity. However, as has always been the case with innovation, the architecture itself needs to have a level of interest beyond that of the showcase in order to influence others. This is where breakthroughs have always been made, as they were, for example, in the age of steel and glass, or in the evolution of organic design (Mies van der Rohe and Frank Lloyd Wright were as inventive as they were architecturally adroit). Wallmakers's innovations in regard to site-specific systems for sustainability, and in its use of as-found and as-concocted materials, were matched by the ingenuity and flair displayed in its conceptualization and construction of Nisarga. Such a nexus is very much the sign of genuine advancement.

ABOVE The ceilings are lined with jute cloth sacking, and the bedroom windows are framed by metal racks salvaged from a scrapyard.

ABOVE AND OVERLEAF The living area also serves as a performance space, with trenches as seating for spectators. The walls are built with the 'shuttered debris wall technique'.

AURAPIN HOUSE

2004
BANGKOK, THAILAND
BOON DESIGN

'In the harsh urban context of Bangkok, I made this house "old" from the start,' states Boonlert Hemvijitraphran. Designed as an exercise in structural ingenuity, as a re-creation of traditional 'Thai-ness' and as an extremely pleasant place to live, the house that Hemvijitraphran built for his young family twenty years ago remains in near-perfect condition. Set well back from the street on a small plot of land in a well-manicured Bangkok suburb, the three-storey house is elevated above ground level and wrapped on its two visible elevations by a contiguous array of folding screens made from rusted steel coated with polyurethane. The slender steel members have aged well, with a patina that appears to be a veritable simulacrum of timber, which, one might say, was the underlying intention. Hemvijitraphran explains, 'This house is very me. I love the Thai and the rustic,' and the traditional Thai houses enclosed by screens to which he refers were, of course, built from wood.

This 'Thai-ness' was not confined to the exterior, as the proportions of the double-height living area were directly derived from those of the Thai shophouse, which had a width of 3.6 metres (12 feet) for each of its structural bays (Hemvijitraphran subdivided those dimensions to create a system of 2 × 1.8 metres, 6½ × 6 feet). The living room is overlooked by a mezzanine supported by a vierendeel truss, meaning that no columns need intrude upon the wonderful light-filled space, and here the overriding structural system is revealed as something clear and simple, yet rigorously resolved. For Hemvijitraphran, 'Structural design is critical. I love it when structure becomes architecture. I am an old-fashioned architect...I believe that structure is the true nature of things. I ensure that a design has a simplicity of form, and that it can be built correctly. The details can come later.' And as he points out, this house may look traditional, but it is also very modernist in terms of the fixed regularity of its modular framework.

Aside from the virtues and inventiveness of its construction, this house celebrates tropicality. On the eastern elevation, the morning sun is filtered through bamboo blinds, which were laid within the vertical strips of the shutters, and the living room

OPPOSITE AND ABOVE As was commonplace in traditional Thai architecture, the three-storey house is enclosed by screened shutters: here made from steel rather than teak.

extends out to a secluded pool-deck with strategically planted trees. Breezes circulate throughout a house where cross-ventilation was integral to the structural parti – the three-dimensional planning – and, in the stifling heat of Bangkok, the ambience is unexpectedly cool and refreshing. Voids on the upper levels between the external skin of shutters and screens and the house serve as buffer zones for insulation and ventilation, not to mention maintenance, and their walkways form a rather singular architectural promenade. Striated and filigreed shadow patterns, which are reflected in the high casement windows, form a captivating display of the inherent visual delights of elemental shading systems, and one might contend that such magical moments are only possible when an architecture is completely attuned to its site conditions.

As Hemvijitraphran is at pains to point out, the architecture is 'humble and low scale, as well as Oriental'. It may be of the twenty-first century, but the architecture is very much of its place, in an almost spiritual sense, as well as climatic and historic. Which is somewhat at odds with Bangkok's current trajectory, where the rudimentary is occasionally enlivened by what might be referred to as foreign forms, and only very rarely by the distinctively local. Hemvijitraphran initially came to prominence with a set of houses completed in the early 2000s that derived from the simplicity and grace of traditional Thai structures, and which also referenced the harmonious disposition – the folding shutters and verandahs – of colonial architecture. The Aurapin House, named in honour of his wife, was to be the last of this series, which, to say the least, is a shame. The house is a wonderful place to visit, and it must certainly be regarded, and learnt from, as a seminal piece of tropical design. Asked whether he would like to recommence his work in this vein, Hemvijitraphran replies wistfully, 'I hope so, I really hope so.'

ABOVE The thermal buffer zones between the house and its external skin contain slender walkways.

ABOVE The double-height living area is lit by morning sunlight, which is screened by bamboo blinds laid inside the steel shutters.

STONE HOUSE

2019
JAIPUR, INDIA
MALIK ARCHITECTURE

So far as architects are concerned, Rajasthan is tropical (as can be said of most of India), but it is arid tropical and has a dry and stony landscape. Jaipur, the capital city, is famed, perhaps even mythologized, for its profusion of buildings and monuments made from local sandstone, but as Malik Architecture points out: 'Over the last few decades, this building material has been reduced to a cladding medium, and its potential as a robust and sustainable structural element is not being explored.' The practice's proposal for a family home on a private estate in an outlying suburb was intransigent, insisting that only sandstone could be used in its construction, and the client willingly encouraged them to proceed. The completed house is quite remarkable, and the architecture does appear rather like that of a public building, but that might just be due to the inherent monumental qualities of rosy-hued sandstone.

Viewed from the street, the three-storey house has a resolutely orthogonal profile, with hand-cut jali screens etched into the façade and sporadically opening out as sets of folding shutters. The thrusting cantilever of the topmost floor signifies the graphic forcefulness of the architecture found within, where the centralized circulation volume forms an assemblage of

OPPOSITE AND ABOVE The east-facing street elevation has a forceful presence, with a thrusting stepped profile decorated by jali screens.

strongly delineated geometries and asymmetrical perspectives. The design language and decorative motifs are aesthetically consistent, and the overall composition presents nothing less than a concerted attempt to reinterpret, and indeed re-express, the fabled tectonic qualities of Rajasthani construction.

The hard Jodhpur sandstone was sourced from a local quarry, and the architects requested that traditional methods of stone-splitting were used – hand tools rather than machines – to reveal the natural qualities and grain. A juxtaposition between smooth surfaces and those hewn roughly becomes part of an underlying and harmoniously controlled set of dualities, where large circular windows loom alongside the sharp diagonals of the walkways and flights of stairs. There is a mannerist touch to the exaggeration and occasional distortion of scale, aided and abetted by an homage to the geometric forms and proportions inscribed in stone by the much-revered architects who worked in northern India in the latter half of the twentieth century.[1] The hand of Louis Kahn in absentia can be discerned in the vaulted ceilings of the living rooms and bedrooms, and most dramatically in those great circular windows.

The Rajasthani architecture of yore was constructed with solid load-bearing walls, and it would appear that Malik utilized the same fundamental method here, but they were in fact erected with hollow cavities. An interlocking system reduced the amount of sandstone required by 30 percent, provided a hidden space for services and, crucially, enabled the provision of thermal breaks, whereby the heat from the external walls could escape through the cavities. As a result of this passive-energy design process, the internal temperatures are in the order of 5 to 7°C (41 to 45°F) cooler

ABOVE The central circulation volume comprises a sequence of asymmetrical perspectives and dynamic geometries.

ABOVE The architecture is both a reassertion of Rajasthani construction and a tip of the hat to the monumental platonic forms of Louis Kahn.

ABOVE Looking up from the basement level. The sandstone walls were built with hollow cavities, as thermal breaks that greatly reduce the internal temperatures.

than those outside. The architects also point out that their insistence upon the comprehensive use of sandstone resulted in other environmental and financial benefits: the method of construction was ultimately cheaper than conventional alternatives; the embodied carbon levels were appreciably lower, due to the relative lack of post-quarry labour, assembly and use of non-sustainable materials; and, as a corollary, the amount of ongoing maintenance required for an unpainted house built of stone is negligible.

Possibly the most salient observation to make is that Stone House looks like a one-off, but it really should not. In an urban context where house construction is currently unattuned to history and tradition, it stands out as an eye-catching anomaly. If, however, it were to be seen in adjacency with other sandstone houses, as part of a suburban collective, it would be strikingly appropriate and very Rajasthani – as if it were ready to be featured in a coverage of global vernacular architecture past and present. The simple point is that with a few tweaks and with the application of technology and science, sustainability can mean continuity, because traditional forms and methods are there for good reason.

ABOVE The gently vaulted dining room adjoins a high-walled courtyard at the rear of the house.

URBANITY AND ATTITUDE

'By becoming an architect, all I wanted was to have a better life...this was not a philosophy, but an attitude.'

BOONSERM PREMTHADA

For all the rose-tinged wondrousness of the arcadian idyll, tropical Asia is consummately urbanized, and, in most of its manifestations, depressingly so. In demographic terms, the twenty-first century has already been defined by the growth of megacities in the region, and all that the phenomenon may portend in an environmental, social and cultural sense. The population drift from rural areas has been unabating, and these cities are very big, and they are getting bigger.[1] In their spread and sprawl, and in their sometimes chaotic and always overheated dysfunction, they are quite unlike anything seen before. Until recently, the motivations that lay behind the design of a tropical house had generally been uninflected by the encroachment of uncontrolled urbanity, but times are rapidly changing. Designs by ethically cognizant architects for a wealthy clientele have been suffused by programs for passive energy consumption – that is now taken for granted, there is little left to advocate, and the end result is effectively determined by the conscience of the client. On a broader scale – one with implications that are sociological and geopolitical as much as environmental – an evaluation of the reasons for building, and for architecture itself, has fomented what loosely might be described as a fresh way of thinking, and most explicitly as an attitude.

The ascendancy of the megacity and the concomitant acceleration of urban blight and climate-related disasters have not exactly created a scenario that might encourage self-referential expressions of architectural delight. The apparently unalterable circumstances are instead demanding practical innovations, potentially radical constructions and, ipso facto, the realizations of a new and different form of beauty. And therein lies the future of urban architectural practice. Vinu Daniel of Wallmakers (see p. 228), based in the Indian city of Trivandrum, has been publicly asking whether we as humans should now be building anything at all, suggesting that the implications of the climate crisis have effectively rendered architectural aesthetics and expression irrelevant.

The questioning, and feasible rejection, of the motivations and objectives of architectural practice in Asian cities has an intriguingly cross-cultural and very recent narrative. In the field of house design, there was little to evaluate – let alone react against – until the 1980s, when commissions arrived from a previously undetected upper-middle class. Initially, for the next two decades, there was little that aimed to reflect – never mind interpret – the genius loci, the spirit of the tropical cities (the preoccupations of Geoffrey Bawa in Colombo, Jimmy Lim in Kuala Lumpur and the tropical modernists of Singapore were essentially site specific). Then, inspired by the only too appropriate tenets of critical regionalism, a sprinkling of intellectually restless architects emerged toward the end of the 1990s, most notably in Kuala Lumpur and Jakarta. They were few in number, but they explained their principles with varying degrees of rhetorical advocacy, and they each built a handful of projects (mainly small houses) that, when publicized, sent ripples of divergence, if not subversiveness, across the region. And yes, it could be said that they had an attitude.

For several years, Kevin Low (see p. 278) and Ng Seksan (see p. 266) worked closely with one another in Kuala Lumpur, and it was an inspiring process of cross-fertilization (quite literally, as Seksan was a landscape architect, among other things). As seen in a set of ostensibly unassuming houses and modest renovations completed in the Bangsar district in the early 2000s, their shared palette of materials comprised roughly finished brickwork, slender concrete slabs, narrow steel columns and totally integrated, yet sparsely vegetated gardens with elegant skinny trees. That palette became a recognizable language, and it signified a new form of architecture within a tropical city, one that was a reaction to and interpretation of the realities of its urban context. Apart from a few grandiose monuments and the rows of surviving Chinese shophouses, the city of Kuala Lumpur had really only been built over the preceding fifty years, and in a most rudimentary style. The built environment was unpretentious, unremarkable and often very grungy, but Low and Seksan proceeded to reinvent it with a hint of the sublime and the picturesque. Both architects have continued to innovate – at a variety of scales and with a range of differing programs – and they have remained very outspoken in regard to

ABOVE Seksan Design, 67 Tempinis, Kuala Lumpur, Malaysia, 2004.

ABOVE Kevin Low, Lightwell House, Kuala Lumpur, Malaysia, 2000 onward.

the ubiquity of delinquent construction habits and unsustainable planning in their city. The ever-prolific and ever-quotable Seksan describes his recent Sekeping projects as, 'inspired by Asia's urban slums. Third-world aesthetics take delight in the imperfections and the mistakes made by workers. My houses are simply knocked together from recycled materials.'

A contemporaneous movement in Jakarta was formalized under the banner 'Arsitek Muda Indonesia' (Young Architects of Indonesia), and aside from any typological assertions or reinventions, the collective was motivated by a desire to respond in a considered and ethically valid manner to the work on offer. A freshly constituted social class had emerged in Jakarta, one that was cultured and worldly, and was able to afford architecture that would reflect a new urban sensibility. The architects were not inclined to blithely imitate foreign styles; they wanted to establish an Indonesian expression, but they had very little to go on. There really were not any identifiably local antecedents in domestic architecture, apart from the tribal vernacular and the houses of the kampongs, neither of which could be considered as emblematic of urban sophistication, and it appears that the collective was quite simply averse to the forms of contemporary tropical modernism, mainly emanating from Singapore. Ahmad Djuhara, for one, did revel in the architectonic re-inscription of a 'shanty' typology when building his own house, but the movement (and by extension, the course of Indonesian architecture) was ultimately given shape by the formal explorations of Andra Matin (see p. 256) and Adi Purnomo (see p. 250). Matin's private houses and small-scale public buildings had a panache and a slyly monumental compositional dexterity that have gone some distance in providing modern Indonesia with an architectural identity. Purnomo was overwhelmingly preoccupied with the problems of how to live in such a vast and unaccommodating city, yet, in the manner of so many resolutely committed architects, he never failed to inject his works with more than a hint of the eccentric and the enigmatic – his reaction to urban existence was always very expressive.

In the often hot and horrible context of the twenty-first-century megacity, it might be observed that a nexus between a not-before-seen expression and typological innovation is tentatively prescribing a new architectural aesthetic. Vietnam has precious little architecture to show from its war-riven post-colonial era, but the last decade has witnessed the proliferation of an identifiable expression, and it is one where the 'look' was determined by a generation of architects who were reacting strongly and decisively to the country's extraordinary rate of urbanization. As Vo Trong Nghia explains:

ABOVE Mamostudio/Adi Purnomo, Urban House, Jakarta, Indonesia, 1997.

'Here in Vietnam, particularly in Ho Chi Minh City and Hanoi, two major cities with populations close to ten million people each, green spaces have become extremely rare. Vietnamese cities lost their tropical beauty. They have turned into concrete jungles like Bangkok or Jakarta.' Nghia himself, through his VTN Architects (see p. 222), has designed as if the cities could be reinvented and rearranged – with the aid of cooperative high-minded human beings – as sanctuaries for wildlife and vegetation. In the hands of several young architects, a fresh Vietnamese aesthetic is characterized in the main by permeable hand-crafted brickwork and idiosyncratic proportions, with an underlying consistency derived from the humility of the programs. The ambition appears to be to do absolutely no more than is required, to do that as memorably and organically as possible and to do it for the benefit of the city. As Đoàn Thanh Hà of H&P Architects (see p. 262), recalls of early setbacks in his career, 'I never gave up, I just kept pursuing ways to put my humanistic ideas into practice,' and as Nguyen Khai says of his design for the Labri House (see p. 218), the 'core value was "close to nature". There are other creatures living inside this shelter, not just humans.'

Rather like earlier projects by Kevin Low and Ng Seksan, the house that Boonserm Premthada of Bangkok Project Studio designed and built for his family in Bangkok is remarkable because it is not remarkable, and it is through

ABOVE Andra Matin, WH Residence, Jakarta, Indonesia, 2006.

ABOVE Bangkok Project Studio, Back of the House, Bangkok, Thailand, 2022.

that attitude of non-assertion that it has gained its currency (see p. 272). There is a somewhat mischievous hint of defiance and a two-fingered salute to the architectural fraternity, but far more than that, there is a hard-nosed intention to design and build for a place and time. Premthada is manifestly not constrained by convention or upbringing, and he claims that he does not wish to design any other houses – he is only interested in the public realm and not people's private lives. And that is an expression of a new architectural reality, one where the city – in this case, Bangkok, with a population of eighteen million – is the world, the environment and the object to be dealt with. Premthada is bluntly pointing out that the life of the city is more important than individual wellbeing, and the architectural presence of his house reflects that outlook – it is of the city, and when you look closely, it is more so. With its rough-and-ready construction and its ungainly proportion, it would go unnoticed by any casual passer-by, but, for those with advance notice and an eye for eccentricity, it forms a 'mannered' reiteration of Bangkok's non-architecture (urban vernacular), and, dare one say, it does suggest and even inscribe a new form of beauty. Premthada states that he became an architect because he wanted a better life, but he was not really thinking about himself – he was thinking about a better life for all. He believed that architecture might be able to do that.

ABOVE H&P Architects, Brick Cave, Hanoi, Vietnam, 2017.

STUDI-O CAHAYA

2009
JAKARTA, INDONESIA
MAMOSTUDIO

In apparent contradiction to the primary characteristics of a tropical house, the only conceivable building envelope presented on a new residential estate in western Jakarta was that of a vertical box, devoid of meaningful exposure to natural elements. As with so many developments in Jakarta's remorseless sprawl, concrete houses are compacted together in serried rows, separated by sheer party walls, with provision for small gardens only at the front and rear. A degree of cross-ventilation can be contrived through that length, but unless manipulated as a structural determinant, it is hardly adequate, and offers little respite from the equatorial heat of Jakarta. Comprehensive air-conditioning is essential, and, rather dispiritingly, so is the need for lighting, as daylight cannot penetrate the depths of a three-storey rowhouse. In such a context, a request to design a house-cum-art-gallery with a bit of verve and swerve, never mind some environmentally minded innovation, could be regarded as something of a challenge.

Throughout his career to date, Adi Purnomo of Mamostudio has been working methodically and exactingly on the thorny problem of Jakarta's unsustainable building practices. As Amanda Achmadi observed of his Urban House of 1997:

> Purnomo incorporates lost practices of passive climatic control that were meticulously pursued in both indigenous architectural traditions and colonial Dutch-Indies architecture, particularly in the making of roof-form. He suggests that, while artificial climatic controls such as air-conditioning are accessible, building design should use passive climatic control by exploring roof forms and creating natural air circulation inside the house.[1]

With the three-level Urban House, Purnomo installed a set of very high walls that channelled air through an open central core and the stairways, with no rooms or spaces sealed off. Daylight is then bounced down these walls through a series of skylights and high vertical windows. Purnomo was utilizing the possibilities of the internal void, which was pretty much the only structural ploy he could engage with in this context of constraint, and in doing so he was not only providing a functional solution, but he was also creating a strongly articulated sequence of architectural forms.

OPPOSITE AND ABOVE Set inside an enclosed vertical box, Adi Purnomo's structural arrangement is motivated by passive energy performance, and ultimately as an artistic expression.

STUDI-O CAHAYA

Studi-o Cahaya, designed for an artist couple with a large private collection, represents a wonderful elaboration on the formulations of Urban House. Hemmed in once more by the rowhouse typology, Purnomo again conceived of a central volume as a sculpted void into which sunlight pours and breezes circulate. *Studi-o cahaya* means the 'study of light', and the architect's structural arrangement was derived from a purely rational assessment of functionality and passive energy performance, which was ultimately extended as an artistic expression. He studied the yearly and daily movement of the sun across the site, and subsequently devised two angles that would divide the three-floor volume in two and admit light through a broad roof-level skylight between mid-morning and mid-afternoon. The resultant series of sloping surfaces contain, support and frame a set of spaces, rooms and exhibition areas that light up or recede into shadow according to the position of the sun and the coverage of clouds. The light and the mood are always shifting, and a completely enclosed house is constantly enlivened by external conditions.

The realization of such a remarkable space was an exercise in how to craft something from the most unlikely, from the most architecturally unprepossessing. That was not done through the use of materials and foliage, or the re-application of traditional construction techniques – as many of Purnomo's other houses have done. Studi-o Cahaya resulted specifically from scientific evaluation, the manipulation of space and above all from what Purnomo describes as 'using light as a material' – and in that expression he is most delightfully enigmatic and philosophical: 'The soul of a house is the most important thing, where the search for light is also the search for the mystery of its shadow.'

TOP AND ABOVE The house is designed as an exhibition space for an artist couple with a large private collection.

ABOVE A large skylight, dotted with pot plants, admits direct sunlight between mid-morning and mid-afternoon.

OVERLEAF Looking down to the ground-floor kitchen. The circular shadows are created by pot plants placed on the rooftop skylight.

IH RESIDENCE

2015
BANDUNG, INDONESIA
ANDRA MATIN

From the inception of his practice in 1998 and the design of the LeBoYe gallery and studio and the Gedung Dua8 Ethnology Museum, Andra Matin has followed an imperturbable trajectory that has not wavered according to presumed typological prerequisites. Matin's houses look and perform like art galleries, and for a certain clientele, those semi-public, culturally attuned characteristics are exceedingly appropriate. As Amanda Achmadi wrote: 'The LeBoYe and Gedung Dua8 projects introduced Andra Matin to a specific section of middle- and upper-class Jakarta: the arts and humanities professionals who were eager to re-imagine a new architectural experience.'[1] Post-Second World War Indonesia had proceeded from President Sukarno's program of national building (1945–67) through President Suharto's implementation of economically driven modernism with First World aspirations (1968–98), and the gradual emergence of an 'arts and humanities' social stratum was to provide the wherewithal, as a client base, for a concomitant emergence of architectural direction and commitment. A fresh architectural expression was shaped by Matin and his peers – such as Ahmad Djuhara and Adi Purnomo, among others – and he was instrumental in coordinating and publicizing the works of Arsitek Muda Indonesia (Young Architects of Indonesia), a movement that flourished to much regional admiration in the early 2000s.

Matin's architecture has assumed considerable prominence through his artfully controlled mediation between tropical expression and elegant modernism, and that sense of balance has been both programmatic and aesthetic. He has reconciled the conflicting ambitions of Sukarno and Suharto, and emplaced an architecture that reflects both a pride in Indonesia's traditions and in its economic and cultural progression. Matin's leanings toward the tropical vernacular are most graphically displayed in the articulation of roof overhangs, the porous continuity of open well-ventilated spaces and a seamless integration with the landscape. On the other hand, the architecture is resolutely orthogonal and uncompromisingly modernist. As seen in IH Residence, the forms, the detailing and the composure of the architecture appear quite Japanese, deferring gently to the likes of Kenzo Tange and Tadao Ando, but the tropicalized dimensions give it a singular expression, wherein the monumentality is leavened by the spareness of the elements.

OPPOSITE AND ABOVE Placed within a large sunken compound on a residential estate, the house is sheltered by a massive roof overhang.

IH Residence is located on the outskirts of Bandung, a large city to the south of Jakarta, surrounded by mountains and notable for a decorous architectural sensibility that lingers from the days of Dutch settlement. The site for the house was quite remarkable, sloping dramatically from the north as an enclosed compound, as a large 'public' garden, and it was that setting of self-containment that directed Matin's design response. Built for a family of five, the house appears to be inordinately large, as if it were a public building centred in a complementary landscape as a museum or a visitors' centre, but the over-scaling is illusory – the architectural language is that of exaggeration.

Encased by massive weathered concrete walls, the entry forecourt is ostensibly that of a palace, but, as is the way in the tropics, the visual austerity is counteracted by the vegetation, by the statuesque treescape. Reached by a long ramp to the west of the entry plaza, arrayed on a perfectly flat ground plane, and mirrored in a broad reflection pool, the living pavilions are conspicuously elongated in plan. The defining attributes of the architectural expression are those of the unexpectedly imposing horizontal layering and vertical repetition, and therein lies the exaggeration. A series of roof forms have a wafer-thin slenderness – that of the main pavilion extends so far that the cantilever appears impossible, but in the context of Bandung, where the rainstorms are tumultuous, this giant umbrella is most sensible. Bounded by the gardens and pools, and sheltered beneath the concrete superstructure, the interior spaces are quietly and humanly scaled, with timber joinery that segues neatly with the off-form concrete. A most enchanting enclosure is to be found to the northeast, where the bedrooms open out to a palm garden secluded below the massive roof overhang. The circulation routes extend as an architectural promenade throughout the levels of the house and the landscape, and up to the heights of the northern boundary, where the entire site-wide composition can be viewed, not just as a house, but as a veritable landmark in contemporary Indonesian place-making.

ABOVE View of the entry forecourt from the south. A ramp leading up through the gardens to the house is hidden behind the wall at left.

ABOVE On the eastern boundary, a palm garden and external corridor are tucked away beneath the broad sweep of the roof.

TOP AND ABOVE The ground plane at the base of the sloping site is perfectly flat, and the architecture is mirrored in a set of reflection pools. **OVERLEAF** The interior spaces are quietly and humanly scaled, with timber furnishings and joinery playing off against mottled concrete.

BRICK CAVE

2017
HANOI, VIETNAM
H&P ARCHITECTS

Across the Red River to the north of Hanoi, the flatlands of the Dong Anh district are being slowly swallowed up by the remorseless spread of the metropolis. This process has engendered a currently curious and strangely disjunctive environment, wherein new and tightly built-up townships are edged by misty rice fields where time has apparently stood still for centuries. Visions of invasiveness are tinged with a sense of melancholy, and as Đoàn Thanh Hà of H&P Architects recalls, 'My client wanted to leave the city and return to his home village to enjoy a peaceful life, but the hustle and bustle chased him back here. The city had penetrated the village.' Ha's design for this small house, only metres from the rice paddies, was an especially expressive piece of architecture, not just in terms of the proportions of its eccentrically yet artfully arranged brickwork, but also in the social, cultural and morphological interpretation of its place, of its environment. The house was explicitly conceived of as a cave, in which Ha perceived that the owner might take refuge and cling to his memories of village life.

Brick Cave has two external walls of permeable brickwork, described by the architect as a 'fence' and a 'façade', which enclose an outdoor space that wraps around the two public frontages of the corner site. Vertiginous, teetering and somewhat illusory, the angular discordances of the walls, beams and openings have an 'Escheresque' dimension, and it is clear that such structural willfulness was patently intended as an aesthetic gesture, one

OPPOSITE AND ABOVE The house is enclosed by two permeable brick walls, which form a buffer zone that filters heat, dust and noise.

ABOVE The earthiness of the façade nestles comfortably in the semi-rural and small-scale industrial context of the village.

that might provoke a romantic, even philosophical response. Brickwork at this scale is used extensively throughout the region for small factories, workshops and farmyards, so the familiarity works both ways – it is local, acceptable and understood, but its use as an architectonic device is undeniably enigmatic. Ha says that he wished to 'evoke a mosaic picture of emotions, that are both familiar and strange…about brick walls, yard corners, the sky, gardens and alleyways. These images are stored in our memory, but they're strange when we meet them again in reality…it's still a brick wall, but it's built in a different way.'

Setting aside its enigmatic and emotional qualities, the house represents a formidable, innovative and, as it transpired, influential piece of sustainable architecture. H&P have gone on to refine and diversify the use of permeable brick construction with a series of larger houses and commercial buildings, and the idea has caught on across Vietnam. Regional crosscurrents might also be noted, certainly in India and Bangladesh, where its usage marks an architectural revival rather than a new direction. The two high walls of baked bricks serve as environmental filters to screen out heat, dust and noise, while encouraging cross-ventilation. While also signifying the notion of 'shelter and refuge', the outside wall – the 'fence' – was canted inward to modulate sunlight and rainfall, and small balconies protrude from the inner wall to support small gardens. The house is covered in vines that flourish in summer, thus adding another layer of environmental protection. The brickwork is continued throughout the interiors, where the material palette is earthy and muted, as befitting a place to retreat from the 'hustle and bustle'.

As demonstrated with Brick Cave, Ha's approach is a salutary reminder of how resourceful and imaginative an architect can be in the face of the relentless processes of land despoliation and cultural fragmentation. He is very much an architect with a social agenda, and his early career had spluttered fitfully as he questioned just how he could realize his ideas: 'Was creativity the decisive factor? Is romance illusory? For whom is humanity needed? But I never gave up – I just kept pursuing ways to put my humanistic ideas into practice.'

ABOVE AND OPPOSITE A flow of fresh air and cooling breezes is stimulated by layered porous brickwork, and by the placement of large openings throughout the structure.

THREE SEKEPING HOUSES

2016
KUALA LUMPUR, MALAYSIA
SEKSAN DESIGN

Having grown up in the old tin-mining town of Ipoh, the son of a traditional medicine shopkeeper, Ng Seksan trained as a civil engineer in New Zealand, before gaining a post-graduate degree in landscape architecture. He set up his own landscape practice in Kuala Lumpur thirty years ago, and rapidly gained attention for his signature stylings, of seductive artlessness calibrated by an impeccable selection of foliage. His landscapes were, in essence, architectural, and it could be observed that they were conspicuously more redolent with contextual and environmental awareness than many of the buildings they had been commissioned to adorn. Seksan never trained as an architect per se, but he has effectively operated as a prolific practitioner for over twenty years now and has become something of a legendary figure in his native Malaysia, and across the region. He unabashedly operates in the public eye as an implacable advocate for that which he believes to be right, and he is loath to admit adherence to a profession he regards not with disdain but with puzzlement: 'Softscape is all that matters in architecture these days, the forms and the beauty are in the trees and nature. The hardscape and the new buildings, they're not the architecture anymore.'

The Sekeping series of houses for rental accommodation was initiated in the late 1990s, and ten were eventually constructed/adapted/reconfigured across Malaysia in an exercise described by Seksan as, 'demonstrating development ideas that were too radical to be accepted by my commercial clients. Sekeping was all about putting my money where my mouth was...I was the owner, architect, landscaper and operator.' The first structures were completed in 2000 at Serendah, in the mountains and rainforests to the north of Kuala Lumpur, as lightweight steel-frame pavilions that floated above the sloping terrain without disturbing the native flora and fauna. The site was then incrementally developed as a gently landscaped compound where the original steel pavilions were adjoined with a set of recycled warehouses and Malay houses. These structures were not just recycled, they were relocated and reassembled on site, with the Malay houses trucked

OPPOSITE The initial structures at Sekeping Serendah are delicately framed lightweight pavilions that do not disturb the surrounding forest. **ABOVE** Sekeping Tenggiri resulted from the conversion of two unremarkable 1960s rowhouses in the inner-city suburb of Bangsar.

up from their abandonment in Johor in 2010 to be transformed by Seksan into luxuriously rustic residences. Cooled only by fans, shaded by newly extended roofs and opened out by the removal of internal walls, the living spaces of the Malay houses juxtapose the original ornate fretwork with rudimentary concrete and raw-brick fittings in a manner that makes a virtue of tactile simplicity, by reverting to the fundamentals and salvaging the vernacular. 'The traditional Malay house is the epitome of a well-designed house. It is humble, comfortable and sensible, and it is beautifully cross-ventilated. But those houses are being torn down every day and sold for scrap wood. I bought these houses for around 10,000 Ringgits each.'

The parti of 'reconfigure, renovate, recycle' was implemented in a variety of developments across the country, and a pair of unremarkable 1960s rowhouses in Bangsar, close to the centre of Kuala Lumpur, were transformed in 2009 into Sekeping Tenggiri, a guesthouse that opens out to a private hillside garden. The conversion is a wonderful piece of design, whether it be termed architecture, landscape or interior design – it is in fact a totally integrated composition of all three. Seksan claims that the design was inspired by 'the urban slums of Asia', but in his hands the paradoxically picturesque and inherently dignified qualities of those neighbourhoods have been reconfigured as what might be described as a set piece of environmental art, comprised of artefacts, curios, water features, recycled timber structural elements and ever-encroaching greenery. To complete the singular expression of contrived artlessness, Seksan's by now well-established architectural language of wafer-thin floating concrete slabs, slender steel poles and roughly laid brickwork, knits all the components together in the indoor/outdoor living areas.

The final Sekeping project, Jugra, completed in 2016, is perhaps the most intriguing. It is not so much a house as a mysteriously evocative environment, where the omnipresent organic entropy of the tropics is embraced and surreptitiously exaggerated. The trees hang low and limp, the ponds are congested by lilies, the brick walls are stained by mould and moss, the sun scarcely penetrates and a languid humidity pervades. Yet it is a charming, captivating place, comprising eight discreet courtyard pavilions and set in an area of Kuala Lumpur that Seksan describes as 'dilapidated', on the Old Klang Road, which once connected the city with its port. The existing 1950s structures were untouched, the new ones were erected without ceremony from brick and slender slabs, the columns of the neoclassical colonnade were formed in a mould found in a warehouse at Serendah, and all else was recycled. The roof tiles had been discarded during the renovation of a

ABOVE The interior spaces of the relocated Malay houses at Sekeping Serendah are gently reconfigured and opened out. Seksan can be seen with one of the kampong dogs.

ABOVE The disused Malay houses were purchased cheaply, then trucked up from Johor to be reassembled as rental accommodation in the mountain ranges north of Kuala Lumpur.

ABOVE Sekeping Jugra is the renovated and artful extension of a rundown 1950s residential compound located to the south of Kuala Lumpur's city centre.

nineteenth-century building, timber doors were salvaged from a Methodist college, louvre doors from a demolished hotel, glass and mirrors from a razed office tower, and the mud walls were made from the on-site swimming-pool excavation. Seksan's retrospective assessment of this amalgamation of unrefined construction with magpie-style recycling is refreshingly candid and revealing. 'I think it encouraged the notion of a Third World aesthetic, where you can appreciate imperfection, where discarded components become architectural features, and where you can get maximum impact with limited resources. The only way to expand design in Asia is to make it cheap and affordable.'

Seksan has moved on from the Sekeping projects, and he is now preoccupied with his Kebun-Kebun[1] movement, which aims to revitalize underused pockets of land in the most densely populated areas of Kuala Lumpur as gardens and farms for the local community. The first of these projects was instigated during the Covid-19 pandemic, when he simply transformed a hillside wasteland beneath a row of electricity pylons while nobody was paying attention. By the time the planning issues had to be dealt with, a farm was thriving, and the local district had been energized to the point where any bureaucratic heavy-handedness would be faced down by popular opinion (TNB, the electricity company that owned the land, had already given the green light). Seksan claims that at least ten more Kebun-Kebuns are in the pipeline, now being championed by community leaders, and he envisages that the entire city will be connected by gardens on currently redundant yet fenced-off parcels of public land. The philosophy that drove the Sekeping series of houses has been applied at the scale of the megacity, and, at heart, it is all about the long-term sustainability of land development and usage through the rational use of labour and resources, financial and social equability, and environmental remediation. It is worth bearing in mind Seksan's role as owner/developer as well as architect/designer when he states, 'The Sekeping developments were principally concerned with respect for the land and the genius loci of the place, and they have shown that taking care of the land and not destroying old buildings can be very profitable.'

ABOVE With its low-hanging trees and moss-covered walls, the languid tropical ambience of Sekeping Jugra is complemented by an architecture of charming imperfection.

ABOVE The street elevation has a rough yet undeniable charm.

BACK OF THE HOUSE

2022
BANGKOK, THAILAND
BANGKOK PROJECT STUDIO

Boonserm Premthada is an interesting, thoughtful, amusing and insightful person, and an ingenious architect who specializes in lateral thinking. He grew up in a low-income district of Bangkok (he bluntly refers to it as a slum), and he quite dispassionately sees his progression toward formal architecture as singularly pre-ordained – not rags to riches so much as just needing to get things done:

> We had no money for toys, and all I had was one pencil and a pile of old newspapers. I had to imagine everything I would like to own by drawing pictures of them. My father was a carpenter, and little by little I absorbed everything, and I kept on drawing. I was sent to a technical school and eventually graduated as a construction foreman. I then studied interior design before I finally got to do architecture. By becoming an architect, all I wanted was to have a better life...this was not a philosophy, but an attitude.

Premthada set up Bangkok Project Studio in 2003, claiming that he did not know how to wear a suit and tie, and that he would prefer to spend most of his time outdoors: 'I need to know how hot, how cold, how noisy and how silent the world is out there.' With the completion of the Kantana Film and Animation Institute in 2011, Premthada claimed the attention of the global architecture world. It is a virtuoso exercise in contemporary vernacular construction, featuring thick rippling walls built from handmade bricks. Coupled with his understanding of craftsmanship, the compositional assurance of the edifice revealed Premthada as a singular talent. Subsequent public projects served to confirm his conceptual originality, and he has been widely and justly acclaimed as an ingenious architect with an evident humanist agenda. Yet he has zero interest in designing houses: 'I don't want to know about people's private lives. I don't want to get involved with individuals. I am only happy when I'm working in public.' He did, however, make one exception, when he designed a house for himself and his family on a small site in Bangkok.

The first thing to be said about Premthada's house is that it is manifestly not a 'trophy house'. As he says:

> We could only build whenever some money turned up. It is not a house to be looked at. We did not bother with the front. It is all about the

ABOVE In a typically dishevelled mixed-use neighbourhood of Bangkok, the house appears as little more than an undistinguished blank box.

ABOVE The bricks are made from fly ash mixed with cement, sand and water, and laid with a thick oozing mortar.

back of the house. And I was sending a message to the city, as the current setback requirements make it difficult to include any gardens, or even a courtyard at the rear on a site like this. So I planned a U-shape to form an aerial courtyard at the back.

The second thing to note is that the house has an unaccountably enigmatic proportion and silhouette, with only half of what would appear to be a steeply pitched gable roof. Premthada explains that he designed a 'half house', one where, rather like his childhood drawings, you need to use your imagination to visualize what the rest might look like. The aerial courtyard, the public space of the three-storey house, was placed as a platform on the top floor above a glazed atrium that rises from the ground-floor kitchen. Flights of stairs run flush to the long blank wall at the front of the house, and this circulation slot – built from off-form concrete and lined with modular metal shelving – is simply treated as though it were a warehouse. As with the street elevation on its other side, this vertical space has a certain rough charm: it is too knowingly undesigned to be mistaken for the work of a non-architect.

Premthada says that the intended aesthetic effect of the completed house was for 'something that is not beautiful, but interesting', and much of that was due to his own 'patented' method of construction. Intrinsic to all his built projects is a novel and experimental approach to craft and construction, almost as though the architect was behaving as a hunter/gatherer, and he is perhaps most renowned for his bricks made from elephant dung, which were used to build the Elephant Theatre. The bricks for his house were made from fly ash (the residue from coal-fired power plants), which was then mixed with cement, sand and water. The bricks were handmade, and, in order to even out the irregularities, they were laid with a thick mortar that was allowed to ooze out on the external walls, creating an image that Premthada describes as in the spirit of older, roughly built houses in the area. It is indeed difficult to see this as a new house – it feels more like a refit of an industrial shell, and one is ultimately struck by the honesty of the architecture and by its prosaic yet inordinately refreshing response to urban realities.

TOP The structure appears to be only half-built, as if a steeply gabled house had been chopped in two and forcibly separated. **ABOVE** Looking from the second-floor balcony into the vertical circulation zone, which is slotted in behind the street elevation.

ABOVE AND OPPOSITE The back of the house opens out with balconies and courtyards, while the set of stairways is sealed off by the blank wall on the street frontage.

ABOVE Taking its name from the 'safari roof' devised by Land Rover for the tropics, the house is shielded from the sun and rain by layers of cantilevered roofing.

SAFARI ROOF HOUSE

2004
KUALA LUMPUR, MALAYSIA
KEVIN LOW

The late 1990s and early 2000s represented a coming of age for architecture in Malaysia and in its southern neighbour, Singapore, especially in terms of what is referred to as 'identity'. Architectural identity should probably be interpreted as the conflation of a manifest pride in the local with a statement of cultural and aesthetic validity. (Both attributes are inherently contentious, but they ineluctably constitute the markers of regional histories.) Kuala Lumpur, Malaysia's largest city and home to its leading practitioners, is only 350 kilometres (220 miles) and four hours' drive from Singapore, but the expression and rhetoric emanating from the two regional centres at this time were most markedly divergent. A thirty-something generation in Singapore had asserted an identity that espoused the clean lines and structural finesse of late modernism, while simultaneously applying principles of low-energy design indirectly from vernacular and colonial precedents. In Malaysia, that same generation eschewed the devotional tenets of modernism, certainly in terms of its streamlined aesthetic, and chose instead to celebrate a contemporary vernacular – the rough, the raw and the gritty. And its most uncompromising and influential exponent was Kevin Low.

Low was born in Johor in southern Malaysia, schooled in Singapore and trained as an architect in the USA before returning to Malaysia in 1992. After establishing a formidable presence in Kuala Lumpur's architectural circles as a lead designer at GDP Architects, he set up his own practice, Small Projects, in 2002, and the impact of his 'philosophy' was immediate and widespread. His initial projects comprised adaptations and alterations to standard-issue post-war inner-city housing stock, and the resultant, seemingly instantaneous transformations were as-new Kevin Low creations. The existing homes had been whisked away and left as shells for a freshly organicized architecture, almost as ruins overgrown by a new fecundity. The two adjectives used most frequently by commentators at the time (and by Low himself) were 'tectonic' and 'phenomenological' – and these works were distinguished in an almost intangible, allusive manner by the tectonic and phenomenological redefining of their context. In purely technical terms, he stripped away all unnecessary structure and impediment to cross-ventilation; exposed all remaining brickwork and concrete; opened up the spaces to

ABOVE A signature of Kevin Low's architecture is the planting of rows of slender, delicate trees in courtyards and gardens.

form an interconnected indoor/outdoor set of urban rooms; and established vine-wrapped courtyards rhythmically studded by the trunks of very slender trees. In purely aesthetic terms, Low was rendering the humdrum iconic.

Safari Roof House was designed shortly thereafter on an upmarket housing estate located on one of the former plantations surrounding Kuala Lumpur, and it was intriguing to observe how he might transplant the principles of his inner-city renovations to the new-build context of the suburbs. Low was not fazed by the demographic disparity – his focus was purely on the architectural. As Anoma Pieris writes, 'The clarity of his structural expression, honesty to materials, and keen attention to detail demonstrates the rigour of [his] approach, which reduced formal agendas to their kit of parts, and explored collage, systemic structure, and regional construction methods.'[1]

The structure of the house is robust, resolute and potentially very awkward, but Low pulls it off, softening the mass of the sheer concrete surfaces with his signature slender trees, and by summoning up an adroit compositional interplay of recess and projection, and permeable and solid. The house takes its name from the 'safari roof' devised by Land Rover for its tropical model, whereby an additional roof reduced solar heat gain, and Low here installed a similar system, with three layers of cantilevered roofing that provide protection from above and stimulate airflow through the spaces between. The vistas throughout the house and its gardens are carefully yet almost artlessly framed, by steel poles, thin concrete slabs and delicate rows of trees, while the details and geometries are assembled in abstraction as a form of contemporary vernacular. As Low recounts, 'A visiting Chinese architect phrased it very well when he said: "Your materials and the ways in which they are fabricated are very raw and rough, but the way in which they are put together is very refined."'

The influence of Low's singular, poetic formulations was to spread well beyond its Malaysian confines. His approach was adapted and localized by a range of practitioners as an environmentally responsive type of twenty-first-century tropical architecture, and as a subtle and abstracted representation of regional identity. Low's personal assessment of the specific conditions and the circumstances in which he has been working are revealing yet elusive: 'The specific context of Malaysia is a difficult one to deal with. It's a lot of everything and a whole lot of not one thing in particular.' He does however go on to say that, 'My inspirations are driven by a response to the driving rains, and that sun which creates a remarkable rate of growth and decay that cakes everything.' The art of his architecture was to be found in that response to an inherently entropic environment, one where he could conjure up – however fleetingly – renditions of harmony and repose in the unlikely setting of an undistinguished urbanized Asia.

ABOVE LEFT AND RIGHT The tectonic juxtapositions of materials and structure are robustly articulated and artfully controlled.

OPPOSITE AND OVERLEAF The voluminous living spaces are devoid of unnecessary detail or ornamentation, relying instead on the poetic expression of an environmentally directed architecture.

a three-dimensional design, where, as he puts it: 'You see the landscape first, you walk under trees, and the architecture is not the immediate focus.' Raising the swimming pool above ground was the big move – this was lateral thinking at its finest – and from that, all else followed. The site was immediately 'decluttered', and a sculpted landscape replete with a canopy of flourishing trees now wends beneath the elevated, elongated pool and an upper-level walkway. To introduce as much scenographic variety as possible on what was essentially a very small site, Mahasom continued to manipulate the components in section and on plan: 'I lifted up the new villa so it was on the same level as the pool, and it could only be reached by a steep flight of stairs. This created a vista of endless gardens, and there was a "flow" through the landscape.' The ground-level landscape leading to the new villa was shaped by a curving pathway, which was bounded by planter beds with low canted walls toned in terracotta. On the upper level, Mahasom was careful to maintain privacy and orientated the rooms of the new villa toward his landscape and away from the neighbours, while 'borrowing' external views that only contained trees. The site-wide rearrangement was, however, not just an exercise in the creation of the picturesque – the new passages, channels, water surfaces and groves of trees stimulated a marvellous airflow, with breezes circulating throughout the gardens and up the slopes.

The other signature design component, or innovation, was the cladding of both the new and old villas with a skin of sparkling aluminium. The surfaces were laid out as horizontal panels with extruded zigzagging triangles, which meant that air could pass freely through the gaps, keeping the walls cool and enabling any heat to escape. The owners have established that the interiors of their existing house are now 6°C (43°F) cooler than they were, and that any residual heat dissipates rapidly at night. The other virtue of aluminium is that long-term maintenance is relatively straightforward – the surfaces do not stain, and any discolouration is washed away by hose. On a sunny day, the visual impact is quite startling – the multitude of protruding triangles gleam and shimmer; and, as to whether that is a quintessentially tropical look, the localized vegetation looks stunning in its proximity.

Perhaps the most fundamental achievement of the reconfiguration was the creation of an integrated compound – as opposed to the addition of a weekend retreat – which was no mean feat, given the constraints of the site and the number of components. With a silver-toned aesthetic continuity, the two houses appear as one, and the demarcation that defines the various particularities of a compound is to be found in the stratification, the layering of ground levels. The notion of a compound as a confined landscape is intrinsically tropical, serving as a communal protective refuge, and it is here achieved by raising, separating and opening out each of the spaces.

ABOVE The swimming pool is laid out as an elongated bridge, crossing over the ground-level gardens between the new villa (left) and the existing house. **OPPOSITE** The original house is also clad in a new skin of sparkling aluminium, which serves as an efficient device for reducing the interior temperatures.

ABOVE AND OPPOSITE BOTTOM The interior spaces of the new villa are directed by the stepping, sloping pitch of the elevated ground plane.

TOP Mirrored in the soffit of the overhead pool, the ground-level landscaping is shaped by a pathway that curves between low terracotta walls.

NOTES

THERE'S NOTHING NEW UNDER THE SUN
Pages 10–17

1 Roxana Waterson, *The Living House: An Anthropology of Architecture in South-East Asia*, Oxford University Press, 1990, p. 30.
2 'Laurie Baker: Architect for the Common Man – An Interview with Gautam Bhatia', *Vistara – The Architecture of India, Catalogue of the Exhibition*, Carmen Kagal (ed.), The Festival of India, 1986, pp. 215–21.
3 Rex Addison in Michael Keniger, *Australian Architects: Rex Addison, Lindsay Clare & Russell Hall*, Royal Australian Institute of Architects, 1990, p. 8.

BRISBANE, DARWIN AND JIMMY LIM
Pages 18–23

1 Charmian Clift in Gavin Wilson, *Beneath the Monsoon: Visions North of Capricorn*, Artspace Mackay, 2003.
2 Robin Boyd in Jennifer Taylor, *Australian Architecture since 1960*, 2nd ed., Royal Australian Institute of Architects, 1990, p. 117.
3 Rex Addison in Keniger 1990, p. 8.
4 *Ibid.*, p. 9.
5 Philip Goad, *Troppo: Architecture for the Top End*, 2nd ed., Pesaro Publishing, 2005, p. 25.
6 Russell Hall in Keniger 1990, p. 92.

ROZAK HOUSE
Pages 24–29

1 Paul Memmott, *Gunyah, Goondie + Wurley: The Aboriginal Architecture of Australia*, University of Queensland Press, 2007, p. 299.

WOOI RESIDENCE
Pages 30–35

1 Houses by Kevin Low, Ng Seksan and the partnership of Wen Hsia and BC Ang, are also featured in this book (see pp. 278, 266 and 176, respectively).

MOOLOOMBA HOUSE
Pages 36–45

1 Taken from 'Architects' Statement' in Haig Beck and Jackie Cooper, *UME 22 – Andresen O'Gorman Works 1995-2001*, UME Publishing, 2011.
2 *Ibid.*
3 *Ibid.*

D HOUSE
Pages 42–45

1 A list of these architects includes Russell Hall, Gabriel Poole, John Mainwaring, Lindsay and Kerry Clare, Rex Addison and Andresen O'Gorman, among others.
2 Philip Goad, *New Directions in Australian Architecture*, Pesaro Publishing, 2001, p. 91.
3 *Ibid.*

CARPENTER HALL HOUSE
Pages 46–49

1 Russell Hall in Keniger 1990, p. 86.
2 *Ibid.*, p. 86.

ADDISON HOUSE
Pages 50–53

1 Addison's architectural and intellectual peer group in South East Queensland comprised (among others) Gabriel Poole, Russell Hall, Lindsay and Kerry Clare, John Mainwaring, Bud Brannigan, Bruce Goodsir, Elizabeth Watson-Brown, Peter Skinner, Gerard Murtagh, Michael Keniger, Don Watson, and Brit Andresen and Peter O'Gorman. By and large, their most significant works were built between 1975 and 2000.

PRECIMA AND SCHNYDER HOUSES
Pages 54–59

1 'Kampong' is the Malay word for village. Traditional kampong houses are built from timber, with gabled roofs, which are often decorated. They are elevated above the ground, and the interior spaces are partitioned rather than walled.
2 At that time, if timber was used for construction in Malaysia, the property could not be insured, so it was effectively outlawed, apart from shacks and sheds. Jimmy Lim's client was an insurance broker, who found a way to obtain cover. The rules were amended shortly thereafter.

BAWA, BALI AND THE TROPICAL RESORT
Pages 60–63

1 Shanti Jayawardene, 'Bawa: A Contribution to Cultural Regeneration', *Mimar* magazine, no. 19, 1986, p. 49.
2 *Ibid.*
3 Anoma Pieris, 'Beyond the Vernacular House', in *Houses for the 21st Century*, Patrick Bingham-Hall and Geoffrey London (eds), Pesaro Publishing, 2003, p. 50.
4 From 1957 to 1962, Donald Friend lived in Sri Lanka. Geoffrey Bawa recalled, 'I invited him to Lunuganga for a week and he stayed for three years.'

WALL HOUSE
Pages 74–79

1 Anoma Pieris, 'The Search for Tropical Identities: A Critical History', in *New Directions in Tropical Asian Architecture*, Patrick Bingham-Hall (ed.), Pesaro Publishing, 2005, p. 30.

LUNUGANGA
Pages 84–89

1 Bawa originally studied law at the University of Cambridge. When he decided to take up architecture, he worked as an apprentice for a local firm in 1951, before studying at the Architectural Association in London, graduating in 1957. Over the course of the next forty years, he became increasingly well-known and has long been regarded as one of Asia's most eminent and influential architects.

MALALASEKERA HOUSE
Pages 90–95

1 Geoffrey Bawa (1919–2003) was Sri Lanka's best-known architect. Ena de Silva (1922–2015) was a celebrated artist, credited with the revival of the batik industry. Barbara Sansoni (1928–2022) was an artist and designer, best-known for her colourful textiles. Laki Senanayake (1937–2021) was a highly expressive sculptor and painter. They each interacted and collaborated with one another – and with a host of other artists, architects and designers, including C. Anjalendran – over a period of decades.
2 The same observation might be made of Bali, where ongoing artistic and cultural creativity is permeated with established images and notions of its tropicality.

SINGAPORE AND THE DILEMMAS OF TROPICAL MODERNISM
Pages 102–07

1 Anoma Pieris, 'Outside the Tropical House', in *Houses for the 21st Century*, 2003, p. 19.
2 *Ibid.*
3 Kerry Hill, 'Introduction', *Architecture Bali*, Patrick Bingham-Hall (ed.), Pesaro Publishing, 2000, p. 7.

HEEREN SHOPHOUSE
Pages 122–25

1 Members of the Peranakan Chinese communities in Melaka, Penang and Singapore are known as Baba Nyonya. They are the descendants of marriages between male immigrants from China and local Malay women. 'Peranakan' refers to a Southeast Asian ethnic group of mixed ancestry.
2 Philip Goad, 'SCDA', in *New Directions in Tropical Asian Architecture*, 2005, p. 95.

TROPICAL EXPRESSION
Pages 132–37

1 Rex Addison in Guy Allenby, *Eight Great Houses*, Pesaro Publishing, 2002.
2 Quoted in Bedmar and Shi, *Romancing the Tropics*, ORO Editions, 2006.

BOND HOUSE
Pages 148–53

1 Philip Goad, *Architecture Bali*, Pesaro Publishing, 2000, p. 37.
2 *Ibid*.
3 The stone was sourced from nearby Java, where andesite had most famously been used to construct the Buddhist temple Borobudur.

TELEGRAPH POLE HOUSE
Pages 176–81

1 Taken from the architects' website, www.whbca.com/our-notes.
2 The Kuala Lumpur-based practice of Wen Hsia and BC Ang is now known as WHBC Architects.

WALLS AND ROOFS – MORE OR LESS
Pages 192–99

1 Ernesto Bedmar in Bedmar and Shi 2006.
2 Before the 1980s, some public buildings erected in post-war tropical Asia responded programmatically and functionally to their context and climate, but the forms and appearance were not notably tropical, apart from occasional sun-shading devices. Very few architect-designed houses had been commissioned before a moneyed upper-middle class appeared in the 1980s (the timelines vary from country to country), and from then on, the beginnings of a genre can be detected – both in public and private architecture. Due to geopolitical circumstance, house design in tropical Australia had pre-empted that emergence, as had the design of several resorts in Bali and Sri Lanka.
3 Laurie Baker (1917–2007), a young architectural graduate from Birmingham, UK, first visited India in 1943, en route home after serving as an anaesthetist in China during the Second World War. He met Mahatma Gandhi in Bombay (Mumbai), who encouraged him to return. He did so in 1945, and, until his death in 2007, he designed and supervised the construction of what he termed 'cost-effective' houses and public projects.
4 In a rat-trap bonding system, the bricks are placed on their sides, which can create a sizable space within a wall. A studied assessment of Baker's technique was commissioned by the Indian Housing and Urban Development Corporation in 1992, and it found that the method was in fact the strongest form of wall construction. Baker had previously only built single-storey structures in this manner.
5 WOHA proposed that buildings be measured according to a Green Plot Ratio, a Community Plot Ratio, a Civic Generosity Index, an Ecosystem Contribution Index and a Self-Sufficiency Index. The Green Plot Ratio measured 'the amount of landscaped surfaces compared to a development's site area', deeming 100% to be the bare minimum.

GREEN BRIDGE HOUSE
Pages 200–05

1 Oliver Wainwright, 'Story of Cities #35: Arcosanti – the unfinished answer to suburban sprawl', *The Guardian*, 4 May 2016: www.theguardian.com/cities/2016/may/04/story-cities-35-arcosanti-paolo-soleri-desert

HA LONG VILLA
Pages 223–27

1 Vo Trong Nghia, 'Designed for Serenity, with Nature in Mind', *The New York Times*, 10 October 2019.

NISARGA
Pages 228–33

1 An isosceles right-angled triangle has two sides of equal length, extending in this case to the north and west from a right-angle at the southeast of the site plan.
2 Wallmakers has a fellow traveller in Boonserm Premthada of Bangkok Project Studio (see p. 272), who is also preoccupied with the possibilities of recycled material construction. Laurie Baker, who lived in Wallmakers's hometown of Trivandrum, should be regarded as the 'patron saint' of such architectural practice (see 'Walls and Roofs – More or Less', note 3).

STONE HOUSE
Pages 238–43

1 A lineage of those architects and their works would begin in 1951 with Le Corbusier's masterplan for Chandigarh. In the 1950s, he designed several buildings in Chandigarh and Ahmedabad. Louis Kahn designed the National Assembly Building (1982) in neighbouring Bangladesh and the Indian Institute of Management (1974) in Ahmedabad. Working mainly in the cities of Ahmedabad, Delhi and Mumbai, several now-renowned Indian architects were inspired by the forms and scale of that architecture, most notably Balkrishna Doshi, Raj Rewal, J.K. Choudhury and Charles Correa.

URBANITY AND ATTITUDE
Pages 244–49

1 On average, as an interpolation of available data, the populations of large cities in tropical Asia have tripled since 1990. In 2023, it was estimated that the population of Jakarta was in the vicinity of thirty-five million, Delhi thirty-one million, Bangkok eighteen million, Ho Chi Minh City ten million, and Kuala Lumpur nine million. Other cities within that population range include Manila, Mumbai, Dhaka, Kolkata, Chennai, Bengaluru, Hyderabad, Ahmedabad and Hanoi. It is predicted the populations of the region's megacities will rise by at least sixty percent by 2050. The Indonesian government is now actively pursuing plans to halt the growth of Jakarta, citing the imminent potential for a catastrophic event.

STUDI-O CAHAYA
Pages 250–55

1 Amanda Achmadi, 'Indonesia: The Emergence of a New Architectural Consciousness of the Urban Middle Classes', in *Houses for the 21st Century*, 2003, p. 33.

IH RESIDENCE
Pages 256–61

1 Amanda Achmadi, 'Andra Matin Architect', in *New Directions in Tropical Asian Architecture*, 2005, p. 199.

THREE SEKEPING HOUSES
Pages 266–71

1 'Kebun' means land used for cultivation – gardens or farms.

SAFARI ROOF HOUSE
Pages 278–83

1 Anoma Pieris, 'Kevin Low', in *New Directions in Tropical Asian Architecture*, 2005, p. 183.

CUCKOO HOUSE
Pages 284–87

1 Tropical Space, based in Ho Chi Minh City, was formed in 2011 by the partnership of Nguyen Hai Long and Tran Thi Ngu Ngon. Their architectural peer group includes, among others, Vo Trong Nghia Architects, H&P Architects, Nguyen Khai Architects, CTA Architects, 1+1>2 Architects, and ROOM + Design & Build.

ARCHITECT BIOGRAPHIES

AAMER ARCHITECTS

Aamer Taher graduated from the National University of Singapore in 1987, going on to gain a Master's degree from the Architectural Association in London in 1993. He founded his own practice in 1994, and he has completed a series of houses notable both for their individual expression and their passive design strategies.
aamerarchitects.com

REX ADDISON

Rex Addison grew up in Brisbane and graduated from the University of Queensland in 1970 and the Architectural Association, London, in 1972. He then worked in Brisbane with Geoffrey Pie and Bruce Goodsir and spent several years practising in Papua New Guinea during the 1970s. Addison's architecture is resolutely non-modernist, delighting in the (re) application of localized vernacular.
rexaddison.com.au

ANDRESEN O'GORMAN

Brit Andresen was born in Norway and graduated from the University of Trondheim in 1969 before moving to Australia in 1977. Peter O'Gorman grew up in Brisbane and graduated from the University of Queensland in 1964. Both academics, they formed an architectural partnership in 1980, the same year that they married. Peter O'Gorman passed away in 2001.

C. ANJALENDRAN

C. Anjalendran studied architecture in Colombo, Sri Lanka, graduating in 1973, before receiving a post-graduate diploma in 1976 and a Master's degree in 1979 from University College London. He designed a series of orphanages across Sri Lanka for SOS Kinderdorf International, and he became well-known for houses that adapted traditional construction and planning to suit a contemporary tropical lifestyle.

ANUPAMA KUNDOO ARCHITECTS

Anupama Kundoo was born in Pune and graduated from the University of Bombay in 1989. She practised as an architect in the communal township of Auroville, Tamil Nadu, India, from 1990 until 2002. Kundoo has subsequently been teaching at architectural departments in Germany, Australia and Spain.
anupamakundoo.com

AYUTT AND ASSOCIATES DESIGN

Ayutt Mahasom graduated from Chulalongkorn University, Bangkok, in 2003, and then worked for WOHA in Singapore and Thailand, and for Somdoon Architects and Architects 49 in Bangkok. In 2013, he set up his own practice, which has completed a sequence of houses defined by geometric compositions and precise façade detailing.
aad-design.com

LAURIE BAKER

Laurie Baker graduated from the Birmingham Institute of Art and Design, UK, in 1937. He served in China during the Second World War, and at the urging of Mahatma Gandhi, settled in India in 1945. He initially designed leprosy centres, and moved to Kerala in 1963, where he took on a multitude of low-cost projects built from inherently sustainable materials. He passed away in 2007, aged 90.
lauriebaker.net

BANGKOK PROJECT STUDIO

Boonserm Premthada grew up in Bangkok, and initially trained as a construction foreman, then as an interior designer, before studying architecture at Chulalongkorn University, where he graduated in 2002. He founded Bangkok Project Studio in 2003, and his architecture quickly came to prominence through such projects as Elephant World and the Kantana Film and Animation Institute.
bangkokprojectstudio.co

GEOFFREY BAWA

Born in Colombo, Sri Lanka, Geoffrey Bawa trained as a lawyer and worked as a barrister before deciding to study architecture at the Architectural Association, London, graduating in 1957. He returned to Sri Lanka in 1958, and over the course of a remarkable career he came to be acknowledged as one of tropical Asia's most influential architects. He passed away in 2003, aged 83.
geoffreybawa.com

BOON DESIGN

Boonlert Hemvijitraphan grew up in Bangkok, where he studied architecture at Silpakorn University, graduating in 1991. He received a Master's degree from the Bartlett School of Architecture, London, in 1996, having already formed his own practice in 1993. His houses display a classical simplicity of form and are clad by clearly articulated screening systems.
boondesign.co.th

BUILDING BLOC ARCHITECTS

B C Ang graduated from the Universiti Teknologi Malaysia in 1998. In 2005 he formed Building Bloc Architects with Wen Hsia Ang, who graduated from the Universiti Malaya in 2004. Based in Kuala Lumpur, the self-proclaimed 'blue-collar' practice is now known as WHBC Architects.
whbca.com

CHEONG YEW KUAN (AREA DESIGNS)

Cheong Yew Kuan was born in Kuantan, Malaysia, and graduated from the National University of Singapore in 1988. He then worked for Kerry Hill Architects until 1994, when he formed his own practice, Area Designs, in order to complete the Begawan Giri resort in Bali. He has since designed high-end houses and resorts all over the tropical world.
areadesigns.com

CSYA

Sonny Chan Sau Yan grew up in Kuala Lumpur before attending boarding school in the UK and studying architecture at the Northern Polytechnic in London, graduating in 1963. He headed to Singapore in 1965 to join Kumpulan Akitek, where he designed several significant projects, including the Kuantan Hyatt hotel. He set up his own practice, Chan Sau Yan Associates (CSYA), in 1993.

DESIGN UNIT

John Bulcock graduated from Hull School of Architecture, UK, in 1983, and travelled and worked extensively before taking up a position with Balkrishna Doshi in Ahmedabad in 1994. He then moved to Kuala Lumpur, where he worked for Jimmy Lim, among others, before founding Design Unit in 2001. His houses are notable for their harmonious use of materials and commitment to sustainability.
designunit.com.my

DONOVAN HILL

Brian Donovan graduated from the University of Queensland in 1985, before working with Peter O'Gorman and with Atsushi Kitagawara in Japan. Timothy Hill graduated from the same university in 1990, and worked briefly with Brit Andresen. Brisbane-based Donovan Hill was formed in 1991, and the practice designed a wide range of projects before merging with BVN Architecture in 2012.
partnershill.com
bvn.com.au

ALEXIS DORNIER

Alexis Dornier was born in Munich and studied architecture at Berlin University of the Arts. Between 2004 and 2007 he worked in New York City, before setting up his own architecture and industrial design company in Germany in 2008. He relocated to Bali in 2013, and his practice, based in Uluwatu, is now known as Alexis Dornier Makings.
alexisdornier.com

ERNESTO BEDMAR ARCHITECTS

Ernesto Bedmar grew up and studied architecture in Córdoba, Argentina, and worked with compatriot Miguel Ángel Roca in Soweto, South Africa, and with Álvaro Siza in Macau. He then moved to Singapore, where he founded Bedmar & Shi Designers in 1986, and became highly regarded for his bespoke houses and resorts. Ernesto Bedmar Architects was formed in 2015.
ebedmararchitects.com

FAHSHING ARCHITECT

Frank Ling Fahshing grew up in Kota Kinabalu, Malaysia, and graduated in architecture from Arizona State University in 1985. He worked in Arizona and California until 1990, when he returned to Kota Kinabalu as a founding partner of TeamConcept Architects before setting up his own practice in 2001. Fahshing passed away in 2011.

GFAB ARCHITECTS

Gary Fell grew up in Nottingham, UK, and graduated from London's Bartlett School of Architecture in 1994. He then worked in Bali on John Heah's Four Seasons Sayan resort and stayed on to form Gfab Architects in 1999. Based in Denpasar, Bali, Gfab has designed houses and resorts across Southeast Asia that prioritize the integration of internal and external spaces.
gfabarchitects.com

GUZ ARCHITECTS

Guz Wilkinson grew up in rural Cheshire, UK, graduating from the University of Manchester in 1985. He then travelled overland to Hong Kong, where he worked for four years before embarking on a series of long solo sailing trips. After winding up in Singapore, he started his own practice in 1995 and is now well-known for his finely crafted, environmentally minded houses.
guzarchitects.com

H&P ARCHITECTS

Đoàn Thanh Hà graduated from Hanoi Architectural University, Vietnam, in 2002 and formed H&P Architects in 2009. The practice has designed a range of small-scale projects directed by traditional systems and principles, and built from natural, recycled and often rudimentary materials.
hpa.vn

JOHN HEAH

John Heah grew up in Penang, Malaysia, before studying architecture at University College London and the University of Cambridge. He worked for Ron Herron for two years before setting up his London-based company, Heah & Co, in 1988. He has been widely acclaimed for his integration of architecture, interior design and landscaping in a series of resorts and luxury developments around the world.

HIREN PATEL ARCHITECTS

Hiren Patel graduated in architecture from CEPT University, Ahmedabad, India, in 1983, where he had also taken a course in art. He spent the next five years studying landscape architecture and interior design, with a one-year stint in Switzerland, before founding his own practice in 1989. All his houses and condominium designs are notable for the integration of gardens with interior spaces.
hpa.co.in

KANIKA R'KUL ARCHITECT

Kanika Ratanapridakul was born in Bangkok, and after graduating from the Southern Illinois University in 1984, she received a Master's degree from Southern California Institute of Architecture in Los Angeles in 1991. Apart from a short stint in Germany, she has since worked in Bangkok, mainly as a private practitioner, and formed Spacetime Architects in 2004.
spacetimearchitects.com

KERRY HILL ARCHITECTS

Kerry Hill was born in Perth and graduated from the University of Western Australia in 1968. In 1971, he began work for Palmer & Turner in Hong Kong, Bali and Jakarta. Setting up his own Singapore-based practice in 1979, he has been widely acclaimed for the design of tropical resorts across Asia. Kerry Hill passed away in 2018.
kha.studio

JIMMY LIM

Jimmy Lim Cheock Siang grew up in Penang, Malaysia, before attending boarding school in Sydney and studying architecture at the University of New South Wales. He graduated in 1968 and returned to Malaysia in 1972, where he worked in Kuala Lumpur before setting up his own practice in 1978. He was to then pioneer a resurgence of interest in environmentally aware design across tropical Asia.
jimmylimdesign.com

KEVIN LOW

Kevin Low was born in Johor, Malaysia, and studied at the University of Oregon and the Massachusetts Institute of Technology, graduating in 1991. He returned to Malaysia in 1992 and worked at GDP Architects in Kuala Lumpur before establishing his own firm, 'small projects', in 2002. His always identifiable architectural expression is focused upon 'the possibility of context'.
small-projects.com

MALIK ARCHITECTURE

Kamal Malik was raised in Shimla, northern India, and studied architecture at the School of Planning and Architecture in New Delhi before founding his own firm in 1976, based in Mumbai. His son, Arjun, graduated from the Rachana Sansad Academy in Mumbai, and received a Master's degree from Columbia University in New York. He joined Malik Architecture in 2005.
malikarchitecture.com

MAMOSTUDIO

Adi Purnomo graduated from the Universitas Gadjah Mada in Yogyakarta, Indonesia, in 1993. After working with PAI Jakarta and DP Architects in Jakarta and Singapore, he began sole practice in 1999 and founded Mamostudio in 2008. Purnomo has been very active in architectural discourse and group exhibitions, both in Indonesia and internationally.
mamostudio.id

ANDRA MATIN

Andra Matin was born in Bandung, Indonesia, and graduated from Parahyangan University in 1988. He then worked in Jakarta for Pt. Grahacipta Hadiprana-Architect before forming his own practice in 1998. His work has been widely acclaimed for its fusion of modernist forms with an innate understanding of Indonesia's heritage and culture.
andramatin.com

NGUYEN KHAI ARCHITECTS & ASSOCIATES

Nguyen Quang Khai was born in Huế, Vietnam, and after many years studying and working across Vietnam, he founded Nguyen

Khai Architects & Associates in 2016. NKAA has subsequently designed many small, finely detailed and environmentally aware projects, both in Huế and further afield.
nkaa.studio

RAHUL MEHROTRA ARCHITECTS
Rahul Mehrotra was born in New Delhi and graduated from the School of Architecture in Ahmedabad in 1985, which was followed by a Master's degree from the Graduate School of Design at Harvard University in 1987. He worked for Charles Correa before forming his own Mumbai-based practice in 1990. Mehrotra is currently Chair of the Department of Urban Planning and Design at Harvard Graduate School of Design.
rmaarchitects.com

RUSSELL HALL ARCHITECTS
Russell Hall grew up on a farm and studied at the University of Queensland, where he failed his third year twice before graduating in 1974 from the Queensland Institute of Technology. He worked for James Birrell as a student, and from 1975 he spent four years in Papua New Guinea. He then set up practice in Brisbane and designed several highly influential and often idiosyncratic projects.

SCDA ARCHITECTS
Soo K. Chan grew up in Penang, Malaysia, and graduated from Washington University in St Louis in 1984. He gained a Master's degree from Yale University in 1987 and worked in America before moving to Singapore in 1990, where he set up SCDA in 1995. Now with offices in Shanghai, Manila, and New York, the practice has completed a wide range of large-scale projects across the world.
scdaarchitects.com

SEKSAN DESIGN
Ng Sek San was born in Ipoh, Malaysia, and studied both civil engineering and landscape architecture in Christchurch, New Zealand. After graduating in 1985, he worked as a landscape architect in New Zealand and Singapore before forming his own practice in Kuala Lumpur in 1994. He is also known for his architecture, adaptive re-use of old structures and urban regeneration projects.
seksan.com

STUDIO TONTON
Antony Liu was born in Jakarta and graduated from Tarumanagara University in 1991. He then worked in Jakarta and Bandung before going into private practice in 1996. Based on the outskirts of Jakarta and specializing in residential and resort work, Studio TonTon was formed in 2007, and was renamed as Antony Liu + Ferry Ridwan / Studio TonTon in 2018.
studiotonton.com

STUDIOMILOU
Jean-François Milou was born in Niort, France, and studied architecture at the Ecole Nationale Supérieure des Beaux-Arts in Paris. He founded studioMilou in 1988, gaining wide recognition for the adaptive re-use of historic buildings. Milou designed the National Gallery of Singapore in 2009, and he has since opened offices in Singapore and Vietnam.
studiomilou.sg

TROPICAL SPACE
Nguyen Hai Long graduated from the University of Architecture Ho Chi Minh City in 2001 and received his Master's degree in 2009. Tran Thi Ngu Ngon graduated from the same university in 2004, and they formed Tropical Space in 2011. Based in Ho Chi Minh City, the practice has designed a range of houses and commercial projects that feature porous structure and humble materials.
tropicalspaceil.com

TROPPO
Adrian Welke and Phil Harris both graduated from the University of Adelaide in 1978. After undertaking a lengthy road trip to study vernacular construction in outback Australia, they set up practice in Darwin in 1981. Troppo has since opened several offices across Australia, and it has not deviated from the founding principles of regionally responsive, sustainable architecture.
troppo.com.au

VO TRONG NGHIA ARCHITECTS
Vo Trong Nghia grew up in a village in Quang Binh province, Vietnam, and studied architecture at Hanoi University. In 1996, he won a scholarship to study in Japan, where he gained a Master's degree and a Ph.D. He returned to Vietnam in 2006 and set up his own practice, whose many works have displayed a fresh, experimental approach to ecologically inspired design.
vtnarchitects.net

WALLFLOWER ARCHITECTURE + DESIGN
Robin Tan graduated from the University of Singapore in 1995 and worked for William Lim and Ernesto Bedmar before founding Wallflower Architecture + Design in 1999 with Cecil Chee. Wallflower has designed a series of distinctively sculpted houses that use fundamental and time-honoured procedures for passive cooling in the tropics.
wallflower.com.sg

WALLMAKERS
Vinu Daniel was born in Dubai and grew up in Abu Dhabi before studying architecture at the College of Engineering in Trivandrum, Kerala, India. He graduated in 2005 and spent two years with the Auroville Earth Institute before returning to Trivandrum to form his own architectural practice, named Wallmakers, dedicated to inventing methods for sustainable and affordable construction.
wallmakers.org

WOHA
Mun Summ Wong graduated from the National University of Singapore in 1989 and joined Kerry Hill Architects, where he met Richard Hassell, who had graduated from the University of Western Australia in the same year. They formed WOHA in 1994 and completed a number of houses in Singapore before going on to design highly acclaimed public projects across Asia and Australia.
woha.net

WOOI ARCHITECT
Wooi Lok Kuang grew up in rural Kedah, Malaysia, and studied architecture at the University of New South Wales in Sydney, graduating with a Master's degree in 1990. He returned to Malaysia in 1991 and worked with Jimmy Lim before starting his own practice in 1996. He has designed a series of houses that delight in craftsmanship and pay homage to vernacular forms.
wooiarchitect.org

CHARLES WRIGHT
Charles Wright grew up in Melbourne and studied both fine art and architecture at Royal Melbourne Institute of Technology (RMIT) University, graduating in 2000. He then worked at Lyons Architects before relocating to northern Queensland in 2004. He set up practice in Port Douglas and has since designed a series of distinctively 'tropicalized' houses and public buildings.
wrightarchitects.com.au

INDEX

PICTURE CREDITS

Photographs © Patrick Bingham-Hall unless listed below.
p. 11: Photo Christiaan Benjamin Nieuwenhuis
p. 20, right: Photo courtesy of Russell Hall
p. 21: Photo courtesy of Troppo Architects
p. 273: Photo © Spaceshift Studio
p. 275, top: Photo © Spaceshift Studio
p. 285: Photo © Oki Hiroyuki
p. 287: Photos © Oki Hiroyuki

ACKNOWLEDGMENTS

The photographs for this book were taken over a period of twenty-five years, and I would like to thank each and every architect and homeowner for their patience, understanding and hospitality. Many of the architects have become longstanding friends of mine, and I am forever grateful for the good times that we have shared. It is something of an understatement to say that these architects have been forward thinkers at a time when that has been urgently required. I hope that my depiction and interpretation of their work serves them well: long may their flames burn brightly and their legacies prevail.

Patrick Bingham-Hall
Kuala Lumpur, December 2024

All project dates show the year of completion unless otherwise stated.

All quotations without notes are taken from emails and conversations with the author.

Front cover: Sekeping Serendah by Seksan Design, Kuala Lumpur, Malaysia. Photograph © Patrick Bingham-Hall

Back cover, clockwise from top left: Green Bridge House by Design Unit, Kuala Lumpur, Malaysia; Samujana by Gfab Architects, Koh Samui, Thailand; Stone House by Malik Architecture, Jaipur, India. Photographs © Patrick Bingham-Hall

p.2: Studi-O Cahaya by Mamostudio, Jakarta, Indonesia
pp. 4–5: Village House by Hiren Patel Architects, Surat, India
p. 18: Lake Weyba House by Gabriel Poole, Weyba Downs, Australia
p. 60: Aman Dari Resort by Peter Muller, Bali, Indonesia
p. 102: House at Hua Guan Avenue by WOHA, Singapore
p. 132: The Edge House by Charles Wright, Port Douglas, Australia
p. 192: Dama zAmya by Design Unit, Phuket, Thailand
p. 244: 67 Tempinis by Seksan Design, Kuala Lumpur, Malaysia

Patrick Bingham-Hall is the author of over twenty books on architecture, urban design and landscape architecture. His books reflect a preoccupation with the relationship between architecture and society, and with the co-existence of the built and natural environments. Both a writer and photographer, he has lived and worked in Singapore, Sydney, Oxford and Kuala Lumpur.

First published in the United Kingdom in 2025 by
Thames & Hudson Ltd, 6–24 Britannia Street, London WC1X 9JD

First published in the United States of America in 2025 by
Thames & Hudson Inc., 500 Fifth Avenue, New York, New York 10110

Cover designed by Steve O'Connell

Interior layout designed by Adam Hooper, www.hoopdesign.co.uk

EU Authorized Representative: Interart S.A.R.L.
19 rue Charles Auray, 93500 Pantin, Paris, France
productsafety@thameshudson.co.uk
interart.fr

A CIP catalogue record for this book is available from the British Library

Library of Congress Control Number 2024935642

ISBN 978-0-500-02701-1
01

Printed and bound in China by C&C Offset Printing Co. Ltd.